GOD'S HALL OF FAITH

Speaks Today

HEBREWS 11

J. DAVID ESHLEMAN

God's Hall of Faith

Speaks Today

Copyright © 2019
by J. David Eshleman

Scripture quotations marked AMP: "Scripture quotations taken from the New American Standard Bible®, Copyright © 1960, 1962, 1963, 1968, 1971, 1972, 1973, 1975, 1977, 1995 by The Lockman Foundation. Used by permission." (www.Lockman.org)

Scripture quotations marked CEV are taken from the Contemporary English Version® Copyright ©1995 American Bible Society. All rights reserved.

Scripture quotations marked KJV are from the Holy Bible, King James Version (Authorized Version). First published in 1611. Quoted from the KJV Classic Reference Bible, Copyright ©1983 by The Zondervan Corporation.

Scripture quotations marked Msg. are taken from The Message. Copyright ©1993, 1994, 1995, 1996, 2000, 2001, 2002, 2003 by Eugene H. Peterson. Used by permission of NavPress Publishing Group.

Scripture quotations marked NIV are taken from the Holy Bible, New International Version®. NIV®. Copyright ©1973, 1978, 1984 by International Bible Society. Used by permission of Zondervan. All rights reserved.

Scripture quotations marked NLT are taken from the Holy Bible, New Living Translation, copyright © 1996, 2004, 2007. Used by permission of Tyndale House Publishers, Inc. Carol Stream, IL 60188. All rights reserved.

Scripture quotations marked LB are taken from The Living Bible copyright ©1971. Used by permission of Tyndale House Publishers, Inc., Carol Stream, IL 60188. All rights reserved.

No part of this work may be reproduced or copied in any form or by any means—graphic, electronic, or mechanical, including photocopying, recording, taping, or information—without the written permission of the author's family.

Library of Congress Number: 2019908270
International Standard Book Number: 978-1-60126-636-1

Published by

Masthof Press

219 Mill Road | Morgantown, PA 19543-9516

www.Masthof.com

THIS BOOK IS DEDICATED
TO ALL WHO ARE CONCERNED
WITH THE MORAL SLIDE
IN OUR CULTURE.

TABLE OF CONTENTS

PREFACE

God's Hall of Faith Speaks to the U. S. A.

HEBREWS 11

Today is the best time in history to be alive. One hundred thousand people are coming to Christ each day. That's more thirty million each year. More Muslims have come to Christ in the last fifteen years than in the past fifteen centuries. While Christianity is expanding around the world, we in America are suffering a decline. Many Christian are discouraged and have lost hope.

According to the National Institute of Mental Health, twenty-four million or 19.1 percent of US adults had an anxiety disorder in the past year. The majority of Americans are anxious about the moral deterioration in our culture. Our prisons are full; violence is increasing; suicide rates are high, and our home life is deteriorating. Public-school teachers are suspect if they use the word sin. Many, especially of the younger generation, believe there is no such thing as sin. Church attendance has declined sharply since 2000 especially among youth and young adults. "Every year more than 4000 churches close their doors compared to just over 1000 new church starts!" (Churchleadership.org).

This is not the first time God is faced with a moral decline by the people he created. God includes Hebrews 11 in the Bible for us to observe how these men and women of faith lived in such a time as ours.

Most every sport has a Hall of Fame, or a place to honor the outstanding men and women of a particular sport. We emulate the Hall of Famers' achievements and pay to see a listing of their accomplishments.

Hebrews 11 is often referred to as "God's Hall of Fame" or "God's Hall of Faith." Faith is mentioned 27 times in this "faith chapter." Hebrews 11 defines faith and proceeds to illustrate faith by listing 17 men and women who lived by faith. The author, Apostle

Paul, desires to extend the list but as the list is too long, he simply adds, "and the prophets."

I have devoted a chapter to each individual in the order they are listed in the faith chapter focusing on how they related to the situation of their nation's decline. Through the book application is made to our American moral decline. Our understanding of God and our faith in him will be enriched as we learn from God's Hall of Faith. Hebrews will help us to learn to live by faith in our Lord Jesus Christ and to permit his light to shine through us.

While there is no definitive agreement as to who authored Hebrews, a majority of bible scholars believe the Apostle Paul was the author. For literary convenience I have chosen to refer to the author as Paul throughout these pages.

Scripture quotations where the version is not marked are from the NIV (New International Version). Other versions I have employed are:

AMP	Amplified
CEV	Contemporary English Version
KJV	King James Version
Msg.	Message Bible
NLT	New Living Translation

This book will serve well for both individual study or group study.

I'm indebted to my wife, Helen, for her unceasing prayers and her many helpful suggestions in writing the book. Thanks to Larry Lemmon for proofreading.

I thank God not only for the seventeen plus witnesses of Hebrews 11 but also the great cloud of faithful witnesses referred to in Hebrews 12: "Therefore, since we are surrounded by such a great cloud of witnesses, let us throw off everything that hinders and the sin that so easily entangles, and let us run with perseverance the race marked out for us. Let us fix our eyes on Jesus, the author and perfecter of our faith, who for the joy set before him endured the cross, scorning its shame, and sat down at the right hand of the throne of God" (Hebrews 12:1-2).

INTRODUCTION

What will it take to find your name on God's Hall of Faith? The book of Hebrews gives us the answer. The first ten chapters of Hebrews sets forth the great doctrinal themes while Hebrews 11 illustrates the practical daily living of a life of faith.

The outline of God's Hall of Faith is adopted directly from chapter 11. Hebrews 11 presents many windows and true-to-life examples of faith of these people who lived in a declining moral situation. It gives us insights into their struggles and victories. It may surprise you that many of the OId Testament characters, including those listed in Hebrews 11, were not always models of obedience as they strived to exercise their faith and trust in God. These men and women were real, transparent and authentic. Their humanness helps us in understanding our battles in our walk of faith as we identify with them in our pilgrimage. Paul concludes this chapter; verse 38, "The world is not worthy of them."

The New Testament has more than 100 quotes or allusions to the Old Testament Scriptures. When Paul wrote to Timothy, the New Testament canon was not complete, so we can be sure he was referring primarily to the Old Testament when he writes, "All Scripture is God-breathed and is useful for teaching, rebuking, correcting and training in righteousness, so that the man of God may be thoroughly equipped for every good work" (II 3:16-17).

Don't Forget the Prophets

Paul lists 17 men and women of faith in this "faith chapter." After he lists the faithful men and women, he says he does not have time to tell about the prophets. The prophetic books are too often the neglected one-fourth of our Bible. Jesus said, just before his ascension, "How foolish you are, and how slow of heart to believe all that the prophets have spoken!" (Luke 24:25). I have devoted a chapter to the role of the office of the prophet and raise the question of modern-day prophets. While all seventeen of the books of prophecy speak to today, for lack of space and to avoid continuous repetition, I have chosen six for our Hall of Faith.

A Better Covenant

It is necessary to point out that the New Testament is the better covenant which supersedes the Covenant of Law in the Old Testament. However, Jesus said, "Do not think that I have come to abolish the Law or the Prophets. I have not come to abolish them but to fulfill (or complete) them" (Matt. 5:17). "Don't misunderstand why I have come - it isn't to cancel the laws of Moses and the warning of the prophets. No, - Jesus came to fulfill their purpose" (Matt. 5:17 LB). Jesus goes on to illustrate five different ways his covenant supersedes the old covenant by saying, "You have heard it said...but I tell you" (Matt. 5:21, 27, 33, 38, and 43).

When Moses came down from the mountain where he received God's covenant, his face was so bright the people could not look on it, even though it was fading. The new covenant that Jesus bought for our salvation far exceeds the old, for it is eternal. It doesn't fade but glows brighter and brighter as we are transformed to the image of Jesus. (II Cor. 3:7-18).

Paul underscores this truth as he introduces Hebrews: "In the past God spoke to our forefathers through the prophets at many times and in various ways, but in these last days he has spoken to us by his Son, whom he appointed heir of all things, and through whom he made the universe. The Son is the radiance of God's glory and the exact representation of his being, sustaining all things by his powerful word. After he had provided purification for sin, he sat down at the right hand of the Majesty in heaven" (Heb. 1:1-3).

The majority of those in God's Hall of Faith are referred to in the New Testament. They help tie the Old and New Testaments together. "Everything that was written in the past was written to teach us, so that through endurance and the encouragement of the Scriptures we might have hope" (Ro. 15:4). After depicting the experiences of the Israelites on their way to Canaan we read, "Now these things occurred as examples to keep us from setting our hearts on evil things as they did" (I Cor.10:6). Jude reminds us we need to contend for the faith. He then gives Old Testament examples of those who departed from the faith and speaks clearly of their punishment:

"The Lord delivered his people out of Egypt, but later destroyed those who did not believe. And the angels who did not keep their positions of authority but abandoned their own home—these he has kept in darkness, bound with everlasting chains for judgment on the great Day. In a similar way, Sodom and Gomorrah and the surrounding town gave themselves up to sexual immorality and perversion. They serve as an example of those who suffer the punishment of eternal fire" (Jude 5-7).

Because of God's marvelous grace in giving us his Son Jesus to atone for our sin, we too can be included in God's Hall of Fame as we put our faith and trust in Jesus. I pray your faith will grow stronger as you reflect on God's ability to rescue fallen humanity in both the Old Covenant and in the New Covenant as we live our life in Christ Jesus.

WHAT IS FAITH?

HEBREWS 11

Paul begins this faith chapter by defining "faith." "Faith is being sure of what we hope for and certain of what we do not see. This is what the ancients were commended for." (Heb. 11:1). We all see that the book we are holding is real. But more real than this book is the reality that the unseen, eternal things are more real. They are more real because all that we hold or see will pass away while our faith will carry us into God's eternal reality.

Faith gives us confidence that our hope in Christ will be realized and the conviction that the unseen world is more real than our present world. "Without faith it is impossible to please God, because anyone who comes to him must believe that he exists and that he rewards those who earnestly seek him" (11:6). "What is seen is temporal, what is unseen is eternal" (II Cor. 4:18). The Christian lives by faith not by sight. (Heb. 10:38; Ro. 1:17).

Faith

Many people classify themselves as atheist or agnostic. If we want to relate to God we must believe he exists. It takes more faith to believe that this world just happened without a designer than to believe God created the world. My wristwatch or my iPhone didn't just appear or come into existence after many years. It had a designer. God is our creator and the designer. (Genesis 1:1). We believe that God rewards those who earnestly seek him. We must believe that God cares enough to respond to our prayers.

Jesus answers every prayer—"yes," "no" or "wait." God answers every prayer for healing—with a physical miracle of healing or even a greater miracle: "my grace is sufficient." This raises my faith level. I know he will answer—he will do what is best—God does not make a mistake or cause us a needless tear. (Ro. 8:28). Jesus rebuked the disciples for their lack of faith. (Mark 4:40).

The Heart and Theme of God's Honor Role Chapter

The heart and theme of God's Honor Role Chapter is faith. Throughout the Old Testament, beginning in the Garden of Eden faith is foundational. Adam and Eve were unfaithful as they chose to disobey God. The prophet Habakkuk left no doubts concerning the importance of faith: "The just (righteous) shall live by faith." (Habakkuk 2:4 KJV). Habakkuk's words are quoted five times in the New Testament underscoring the centrality of the message of faith throughout God's Word. Faith is the theme of the book of Romans. "In the gospel a righteousness from God is revealed, a righteousness that is by faith from first to last, just as it is written: "The righteous will live by faith." (Romans 1:17). Paul admonishes us to "fight the good fight of faith" (I Tim. 6:12). "Faith and knowledge rests on the hope of eternal life" (Titus 1:2). "We live by faith, not by sight" (II Cor. 5:7).

If you believe or express faith that God exists in today's public classrooms many non-Christians consider you naïve or bigoted. We believe our God has standards: some things are right and some things are wrong. People do not want to be accountable to a God who condemns their unbelief and freedom to live without restraint. Therefore, they, like little children, deny God's exists.

Today the non-Christian lives to enjoy life and good times. Solomon expressed this philosophy in the book of Ecclesiastes. He possessed more wealth than anyone—2.2 trillion dollars. Along with his 700 wives plus concubines, he gained recognition in owning more land and controlling most of the people in the then-known world. According to the Amplified Bible Solomon repeats thirty-three times in the twelve chapters, "all this is meaningless, useless, empty and an exercise in futility."

Living for pleasure, wealth, and recognition results in making ourselves god. We tell God what we want him to do. If God doesn't jump to our demands or do what we desire we write him off.

For God to be God we must let him lead. We let him tell us how to live. "For I know the plans I have for you," declares the

Lord, "plans to prosper you and not to harm you, plans to give you hope and a future" (Jer. 29:11). In following his Word, we find peace (John 14:27) and joy (John 15:11) that no one will ever find in living for themselves. Without God, America is on a downhill moral slide.

"According to a new survey from Public Religion Research Institute, 65 percent of young people in America agree that abortion should be legal in most or all cases. Seventy-three percent of Americans support euthanasia. According to Pew Research Center, acceptance of gay marriage continues to rise in our culture, growing from 35 percent in 2001 to 62 percent today. Only 31 percent of American adults think homosexuality should be discouraged. We could discuss pornography, sex outside of marriage, drug and alcohol abuse, or a host of other issues. The bottom line would be the same: our culture clearly needs moral and spiritual awakening."[1]

What Characterizes God's Honor Role

The basic standard that characterizes one who is to on God's honor role is their faith. The Amplified Bible expands our understanding of faith. "Now faith is the assurance (the confirmation, the title-deed) of the things [we] hope for, being the proof of things [we] do not see and the conviction of their reality—faith perceiving as real fact what is not revealed to the senses. For by [faith], and trust and holy fear born of faith, the men of old had divine testimony borne to them and obtained a good report" (Heb. 11:1-2 Amp).

Faith Is a Verb

Faith is a verb. Knowing about God without obeying God is not faith. The devil believes (or has faith) in God but is lost because he does not obey God. (James 2:19). Our faith is based on Jesus Christ and his atonement. This faith leads to doing good works. Faith and works must be one; they are couplets. "Faith by itself, if it is not accompanied by action, is dead... Do not merely listen to the word,

---

1 Jim Denison's blog, May 8, 2018.

and so deceive yourselves. Do what it says" (James 1:17, 22). Paul concludes his letter to the Romans: "This message is made known to all Gentiles so that they might believe (have faith) and obey Christ" (16:27 NLT).

America has chosen to turn its back on God. We have chosen to remove God from our minds and from our public life. We think and act as if God does not exist. We have made ourselves god and boast in our achievement. We try to convince ourselves we are in control. We decide what is right or wrong for ourselves. Others have no right to question our position. When there is conflict with our opinions or convictions, our culture decided the majority opinion becomes the practice. When the minority does not follow conflict arises. Tomorrow the majority opinion may change. If anyone questions your opinion, they are judgmental, disrupting and hindering the flow of life for America. We used to respect each other's opinion even though we disagreed with it.

Our educators frequently tell us to have faith in ourselves. The problem is, we never live up to what we know we should do. The result is discouragement, depression, anger, guilt and much more. When faith in ourselves doesn't work, we turn to the god of science which is in constant flux as we discover new dimensions we didn't know existed. What we see with our eyes and experience is the only thing that is real for those without faith. But the problem is the "real" or visual does not satisfy for long. We need something more satisfying. We search and find all is vanity and chasing after wind. We are running on empty. Depression is common as suicides continue to increase. We try to appease ourselves with pleasure—a new movie, free sex, video games, drugs, money, fame, but nothing satisfies for long. There is a god-sized vacuum in every one of us. (Pascal).

With science as our god most Americans including Christians live a materialistic lifestyle focusing on things they can see or things that will gain them recognition. They are occupied with their day to day living giving little thought to what follows after death. Many have convinced themselves there is no life after death. Jesus said if we trust in him we have eternal life. (John 3:16).

Faith Is Eternal

Science has proven beyond reasonable doubt again and again that the claims of scripture are verifiable. Many books on near death experiences, e.g. "Imagine Heaven" by John Burke give first-hand accounts of those who have died and experienced life after death.[2] Since we can't understand or imagine heaven, we focus on life here. One of the greatest secrets of the persons in God's Hall of Fame is that, "All these people were still living by faith when they died. They did not receive the things promised; they only saw them and welcomed them from a distance. And they admitted that they were aliens and strangers on earth. People who say such things show that they are looking for a country of their own. If they had been thinking of a country they had left, they would have had opportunity to return. Instead, they were longing for a better country - a heavenly one. Therefore, God is not ashamed to be called their God, for he has prepared a city for them." (Heb. 11:13-16).

Living with a focus on heaven is one of the greatest incentives we have for serving Jesus. The most effective citizens are those who have a strong faith in God's eternal future. They are selfless, living with confidence, peace, security and are free to help others. Listen to the concluding verses of our faith chapter.

Paul concludes: "What shall I say? I do not have time to tell about Gideon, Samson, Jephthah, David, Samuel and the prophets, who through faith conquered kingdoms, administered justice, and gained what was promised; who shut the mouths of lions, quenched the fury of the flames, and escaped the edge of the sword; whose weakness was turned to strength; and who became powerful; in battle and routed armies. Women received back their dead, raised to life again. Others were tortured and refused to be released, so that they might gain a better resurrection. Some faced jeers and flogging, while still others were chained and put in prison. They were stoned; they were sawed in two; they were put to death by the sword. They went about in sheepskins and goatskins, destitute, persecuted and mistreated—the world was not worthy of them... these are all commended for their faith" (Heb. 11:32-39).

---

2 John Burke, Baker Books, Grand Rapids, Michigan, 2015.

As we look at God's men and women of faith in Hebrews 11 may our faith grow so the Lord will say to us "well done good and faithful servant… enter into the joy of the Lord. (Matthew 25:23 KJV).[3]

Throughout this book we will endeavor to expand our understanding of faith as it is illustrated in the lives of these Old Testament heroes. The attempt has been to apply these examples of faith to our everyday life in the 21st century.[4]

---

[3] For further exposition of "faith" see the chapter on Noah, section "Little Faith" and "Great Faith."

[4] For a brief treatment of Faith and the Prosperity Gospel see the chapter on Amos.

ABEL

First Martyr for Truth

HEBREWS 11:4

"By faith Abel offered God a better sacrifice than Cain did. By faith he was commended as a righteous man, when God spoke well of his offerings. And by faith he still speaks, even though he is dead" (Heb. 11:4).

Adam and Eve spent time relating to their young sons the joy and delightful memories of walking and talking with God in their beautiful Garden of Eden. The pictures they "painted" for Abel and Cain: life was perfect, no weeds, no insects, no arguments, anger, or sacrifices. The boys listened and questioned: "What happened? Why can't it be like that today?" (Genesis 3). As they were weeding the garden Cain asked, "Why are there weeds?"

Adam and Eve explained how Satan came so slyly in the form of a serpent and persuaded them to taste the fruit from the forbidden tree in the garden. Weeds were only one example of the terrible consequences of their disobedience to God's command. Before they disobeyed there were no weeds, now weeds grew everywhere.

As the boys grew, Eve repeated their experiences in the garden many times. She told them Satan promised we would not be cut off from God's presence. Instead our eyes would be opened. We would be like God knowing the difference between good and evil. This sounded good. But Satan deceived us. After eating the fruit, we felt guilt and shame. For the first time we saw ourselves as naked. I designed a covering using fig leaves but God was not pleased. Instead God made garments of skin for us to wear. Our sin could only be atoned by the gift of life.

This was the beginning of the sacrificial system that God put in place throughout the Old Testament. Blood had to be shed to cover sin. (Lev. 17:11). In the New Testament God gave his only son, Jesus, as the perfect Lamb of God to atone for our sin.

Abel understood the concept of animal sacrifice while Cain chose to ignore what God was trying to teach. He chose to go his own way in choosing an offering to God. He resented God telling him what to do. "The heart is deceitful above all things, and it is exceedingly perverse and corrupt and severely, mortally sick! Who can know it - perceive, understand, be acquainted with his own heart and mind?" (Jer. 17:9 Amp). Jesus said, "Out of the heart come evil thoughts (reasonings and disputing and designs) - such as murder, adultery, sexual vice, theft, false witnessing, slander and irreverent speech" (Matt. 15:19 Amp).

At harvest time Cain brought a gift from the crops he had cultivated, however Abel followed God's plan and brought several choice lambs from the best of his flock for his sacrifice. The Lord accepted Abel's offering but he did not accept Cain's. Cain was angry. "The Lord said to Cain, 'Why are your angry? Why is your face downcast? If you do what is right, will you not be accepted? But if you do not do what is right, sin is crouching at your door: It desires to have you, but you must master it.'" (Gen. 4:6-7).

Cain was jealous of Abel. His jealousy led to resentment, anger, depression and eventually murder. (Gen. 5:4-5). Cain said to his brother, "Let us go out to the field. And when they were in the field, Cain rose up against Abel his brother and killed him." God asked Cain, where is Abel? He lied, saying he did not know. God cursed Cain. (Gen. 5:8-12).

Today people like Abel choose to worship the way they desire. They may go to church, give in the offerings but the Lord see their proud, disobedient heart. Disobedience leads to death. (Rom. 6:23). What does God see in your heart? Are you willing to pray with David, "Search me, O God, and know my heart; test me and know my anxious thoughts. See if there is any offensive way in me, and lead me in the way everlasting" (Ps. 139:23-240). "Lord, I will do what you ask? I surrender to your will. You are my Lord."

Dealing with Anger

Too often anger moves from disappointment, to depression, loneliness, unforgiveness, hatred and even murder. Recognize your feelings of anger, ask God's forgiveness and fill your mind with wholesome thoughts. However, there are times when it is appropriate to be angry. When your neighbor is passing out drugs to children, when someone is breaking up a marriage because of infidelity or brutality, when innocent people, especially children, are harmed, it's time to be angry. Ask for God's wisdom to know how to respond as Jesus did. Jesus' anger was controlled. It was a righteous reaction to sin. Jesus was angry at the hardness of heart of the Pharisees because they kept people out of the Kingdom of God with their man-made rules. (Mark 3:5). We call these strong feelings righteous indignation.

The Pharisees knew the Scriptures, but they did not apply the Scripture to their daily life. Jesus said to them: "You study the Scriptures diligently because you think that in them you will have eternal life. These are the very Scriptures that testify about me, yet you refuse to come to me that you may have life" (John 5:39-40). "When angry do not sin; do not ever let your wrath - your exasperation, your fury or indignation—last until the sun goes down. Leave no [such] room or foothold for the devil—give no opportunity to him." (Eph. 4:26-27 Amp).

It goes back to our will—do I want God's will or must I have my own self-centered will? Cain's egotistical spirit was never broken. Abel learned to obey and submit to God's way. "My sacrifice (the sacrifice acceptable) to God is a broken spirit; a broken and contrite heart—broken down with sorrow for sin and humbly and thoroughly penitent—such, O God, you will not despise." (Ps. 51:17 Amp). Cain was rebellious while Abel was humble, teachable and had a broken and contrite heart.

Today I work with many of the younger generation that have never learned to obey God. Parents, because of their insecurity or laziness, let the children do as they please. Parents take the easy way of saying "yes" to whatever the child wants rather than exercising loving but firm discipline. The result is that many are rebellious, believing they are entitled to an easy life. Children need parents who love, discipline them and teach them to obey. A child that is taught to obey his parents will find it much easier to trust and obey God.

Obedience is an absolute essential in being included on God's Role of Faith. Abel was included in God's Role of Faith because his faith led to works. Jesus said, "If you love me you will obey me."

(John 14:15). Obedience, which is mentioned nearly three hundred times in the bible is a couplet to faith. They must not be separated.

Hebrews 11:4 reminds us that even though Abel died, his faith and obedience speak to us today. God shows love to a thousand generations of those who love him and keep his commandments. (Exodus 20:5). Like Abel, our good deeds speak today and will continue into eternity.

ENOCH

Walking with God

HEBREWS 11:5-6

After Cain sinned by killing his brother Abel, he went from the presence of the Lord in the land of Nod, east of Eden. Cain married one of Adam and Eve's daughters or granddaughters. They bore a son and named him Enoch. "It would have been possible for Adam and Eve, in the more than 100 years that may have elapsed since their union, to have had over 32,000 descendants at the time Cain went to Nod, all of them having sprung from Cain and Abel who married their sisters."[5]

"Enoch walked [in habitual fellowship] with God after the birth of Methuselah 300 years and had other sons and daughters. So, all the days of Enoch were 365 years. And Enoch walked [in habitual fellowship] with God; and he was not, for God took him [home with him]." (Gen. 5:22-24 Amp).

"Enoch was taken from this life, so that he did not experience death: He could not be found, because God had taken him away. For before he was taken, he was commended as one who pleased God" (Heb. 11:5). Verse 6 explains how we can walk with God. Note that it begins with the conjunction, "and". "And without faith it is impossible to please God, because anyone who comes to him must believe that he exists and that he rewards those who earnestly seek him." Faith is the key to walking with God. We cannot separate biblical faith with obedience to God.

Walking with God Involves Our Will

Paul explains how we are able to overcome sin. "It is God who is all the while effectively at work in you - energizing and creating in

---

5 See footnote in Amplified Bible under Genesis 4:17.

you the power and desire - both to will and to work for His good pleasure and satisfaction and delight" (Philippians 2:13 Amp).

David walked with God, "Blessed, happy, fortunate and to be envied are the undefiled - the upright, truly sincere and blameless - in the way [of the revealed will of God]; who walk, that is, order their conduct and conversation—in [the whole of God's revealed will] the law of the Lord." (Ps. 119:1 Amp). The Godly walk in his ways. (v.3). "With my whole heart have I sought You, inquiring for and of You, and yearning for You; O let me not wander or step aside [either in ignorance or willfully] from Your commandments." (v.10). David continues, "Establish my steps and direct them by (means of) Your word." (v.133). "The steps of a [good] man are directed and established of the Lord, when He delights in his way [and He busies himself with his every step]. (Psalm 37:23-24 Amp.). Take the word "luck" out of your vocabulary. Recognize God in your midst and thank him. Only those who follow Christ will truly know Christ.

Paul admonishes the Galatian church to, "walk and live habitually in the (Holy) Spirit - responsive to and controlled and guided by the Spirit; then you will certainly not gratify the cravings and desires of the flesh—of human nature without God. For the desires of the flesh are opposed to the (Holy) Spirit, and the [desires of the] Spirit are opposed to the flesh (Godless human nature); for these are antagonistic to each other continually withstanding and in conflict with each other - so that you are not free but are prevented from doing what you desire to do... The doing (practices) of the flesh are clear—obvious: they are immorality, impurity, indecency, idolatry, sorcery, enmity, strife, jealousy, anger (ill temper), selfishness, divisions (dissensions), party spirit (factions, sects with peculiar opinions, heresies), envy, drunkenness, carousing, and the like. I warn you beforehand, just as I did previously, that those who do such things shall not inherit the kingdom of God. But the fruit of the (Holy) Spirit, [the work which His presence within accomplishes]—is love, joy (gladness), peace, patience (an even temper, forbearance), kindness, goodness (benevolence), faithfulness (meekness, humility), gentleness, self-control (self-restraint,) ... Those who belong to Christ Jesus, the Messiah, have crucified the flesh - the Godless human nature - with its passions and appetites and desires. If we live by the (Holy) Spirit, led also walk by the Spirit.—If by the (Holy) Spirit we have our life in God, let us go forward walking in line, our conduct controlled by the Spirit" (Gal. 5:16-25 Amp).

The Galatian Church did not heed this message because Paul had to repeat it. (v. 21). Walking with God is possible only via the Holy Spirit who dwells in you. We are told approximately two hundred times in the New Testament that Jesus is in us and we are in him. Jesus invites us to walk with him. "Come to Me, all you who labor and are heavy-laden and overburdened, and I will cause you to rest - I will ease and relieve and refresh your souls. Take my yoke upon you and learn of Me; for I am gentle (meek) and humble (lowly) in heart, and you will find rest - relief, ease and refreshment and recreation and blessed quiet—for your souls. For My yoke is wholesome (useful, good) - not harsh, hard, sharp or pressing, but comfortable, gracious and pleasant; and My burden is light and easy to be borne." (Matt. 11:28-30 Amp).

Just as Jesus came to do not his will but the will of the Father we are to walk with him, to deny our self-centered, narcissistic will and invite Jesus to take control of our will. Jesus was one with his Father so he could say, "I only say what the Father tells me to say and do only what the Father tells me to do." (John 5:19; 12:49-50). As we mature in our walk with Jesus we too will learn to say and do only what the he wants us to say and do. We will never be perfect as Paul explains, "Not that I have already obtained all this, or have already been made perfect, but I press on to take hold of that for which Christ Jesus took hold of me. Brothers, I do not consider myself to have taken hold of it. But one thing I do, forgetting what is behind and straining toward what is ahead, I press on toward the goal to win the prize for which God has called me heavenward in Christ Jesus" (Phil. 3:12-14).

Loving God Is Supreme

God wants our fellowship. He wants to speak to us and wants to hear from us. "Learning to hear God is much more about becoming comfortable in a continuing conversation and learning to constantly lean on the goodness and love of God, than it is about turning God into an ATM for advice or treating the Bible as a crystal ball." Willard notes that the ultimate question is not whether we are hearing from God but whether we are in love with him. Our concern for discerning God's voice must be overwhelmed by and lost in our worship and adoration of him and in our delight in his creation and his provision for our whole life... Are you in love with the God who is in love with you?... Make loving God your foundational definition of success and the motive for all you do in life. Otherwise, what you do will be "a noisy gong or a clanging cymbal" (1 Cor. 13:1) ...."[6]

When life is routine and ordinary we have doubts about God. Day after day we get up, read our Bible, eat our breakfast, go to work doing the same routine year after year. We pray but see little results. We question like John the Baptist, is Jesus really my Messiah? Is he hearing my prayers. It seems nothing is happening. The supernatural seems far from natural and we are not mounting up as eagles riding on the wind currents of the Holy Spirit.

It takes time to learn to walk in God's stride. Learning to hear his voice is challenging because we are so busy focusing on our life, our desires, our goals, and ambitions. We must take time to hear the still whisper of his Holy Spirit. As David writes, "Be still and know that I am God." (Ps. 46:10). Unless we are still, calm down and meditate, we will not be aware of his calming presence. "God is not going to tell you what he is going to do—He reveals to you who he is."[7]

Discipline is No Option

To stay in stride with God as Enoch we must allow God to discipline us. Even Jesus had to learn obedience. (Heb. 5:8). We must daily choose to take up our cross—deny ourselves, bend our wills to his will. We do not learn to do that overnight. But when we come to walk with Jesus, we experience the supernatural becoming natural. The people we meet, the words we say are directed by His Holy Spirit. There is nothing more delightful, fulfilling or thrilling. Tell Jesus, "I will do and be whatever you want me to be and do and go wherever you want me to go." God's ways are learned in our daily walk, in the routine of life.

---

6 Jim Denison in his June 7, 2018 blog highlights Dallas Willards' words.

7 Oswald Chambers, *My Upmost for His Highest*. Discovery House Publishers, Rand Rapids, MI, Devotional Reading for January 2.

Summary of Walking with God

First, the Bible is our roadmap, our foundation for walking with God. Ask the Father to speak to you now as you focus and wait on him. "The word of God is living and active. Sharper than any double edge sword... It penetrates and judges the thoughts and attitudes of the heart" (Heb. 4:12). David said, "I have hidden your word in my heart that I might not sin against you" (Ps. 119:11). "Your word is a lamp to my feet and a light to my path" (Ps. 119:105).

We can also find inspiration from good Christian books, but learning to walk with God is more experiential than intellectual or cognitive reasoning. We learn by walking with Jesus in our ordinary living. Be all that Jesus wants you to be just where you are no matter how insignificant you feel in your position.

Second, see God in creation. "Every cloud is a flag to God's faithfulness" (Ps. 108:4 Msg). I love to look at the heavens and see God's indescribable clouds. "The heavens declare the glory of God..." (Psalm 19:1-4). Take time to see the beauty of the flowers, the stamp of his love on every person. Pray to see everyone as God sees them. He saw the prostitutes, the tax collectors, the self-righteous Pharisees from God's perspective. God can do the same for you. "God does not want anyone to perish but everyone to come to repentance" (II Pet. 3:9).

Third, see God in your circumstances. "Pray that God may open the door for our message, so that we may proclaim the mystery of Christ, for which I am in chains... Make the most of every opportunity" (Colossians 4:3-6 and Rev 3:8).

Fourth, walk with God in the power of his Holy Spirit. The Spirit lives in you. (I Cor. 3:16). "People who do not have the Spirit of Christ in them don't belong to him... Only those people who are led by God's Spirt are his children" (Rom. 8:9 and 14). Jesus wants to be more intimate with you than your best friend. "You are my friends if you do what I command" (John 15:14). The Spirit prays for you and he will never leave you. (Ro. 8:34; Heb. 13:5).

Fifth, keep in step with the Spirit. (Gal. 5:25).

Walking with God, you will change your world. Walking with God he will transform you (I Cor. 5:17), he will transform your home, (Joshua 24:15). He will use you to change your peers at work.

(Eph. 6:5-9). He will send you to the ends of the earth to make disciples. Jesus commissioned us, "All authority in heaven and on earth has been given to me. Therefore, go and make disciples of all nations..., You will receive power when the Holy Spirit comes on you; and you will be my witnesses in Jerusalem (at home), and... to the ends of the earth" (Matt. 28:18-20; Acts 1:8).

A Focused Life

It takes a focused life to remember God's presence is always with us. "Let your character or moral disposition be free from love of money - [including] greed, lust and craving for earthly possessions - and be satisfied with your present [circumstances and with what you have]; for He (God) Himself has said, I will not in any way fail you nor give you up nor leave you without support. [I will] not, [I will] not, [I will] not in any degree leave you helpless, nor forsake nor let 'you down. 'relax my hold on you'—Assuredly not." (Heb. 13:5 Amp). The triple, "I will not," emphasizes this promise. It is a direct translation of the Greek. The longer you walk with Jesus the more you move from one degree of glory to another. (II Cor. 3:18). There is no such thing as luck or coincidence, rather the supernatural becomes natural.

"Outside of Christ, I am only a sinner, but in Christ, I am saved. Outside of Christ, I am empty; in Christ, I am full. Outside of Christ, I am weak; in Christ, I am strong. Outside of Christ, I cannot; in Christ, I am more than able. Outside of Christ, I have been defeated; in Christ, I am already victorious. How meaningful are the words, 'In Christ.'"? [8]

Walking or Working for God

Before we leave Enoch, let me point out the difference of walking with God and working for God. Working or serving your wife is one level of commitment. Walking with her, that is knowing her heart is a much deeper level. You can buy everything you can possibly think of for her but she wants more. She wants your heart. The same

---

8 Watchman Nee, quoted by Jim Denison on his blog, Feb. 5, 2018.

is true with your relationship with God. Working for God is easier than walking with God. Many work for God, few work with God or walk with God in loving friend relationship. We get tired and worn out when we work for God. It's easy to confuse religious activity, i.e. working in place of for spiritual fellowship. God is with us, in us, walking beside us. It's helpful that we see ourselves with (side by side) more than working for God. We learn to move from servants to friends walking with our Older Brother, Jesus. (John 15:15)

NOAH

Exhibited a Boat Load of Faith

HEBREWS 11:7

"By faith Noah, when warned about things not yet seen, in holy fear built an ark to save his family. By his faith he condemned the world and became heir of the righteousness that comes by faith" (Heb. 11:7).

Noah became the father of Shem, Ham, and Jepheth. Afterward "the Lord saw that the wickedness of man was great in the earth, and that every imagination and intention of all human thinking was only evil continually, and the Lord regretted that he had made man and was grieved at heart. So, the Lord said, I will destroy, blot out and wipe away mankind whom I have created… not only man, [but] the beast and the creeping things and the birds of the air, for it grieves and makes me regretful that I have made them. But Noah found favor in the eyes of the Lord... for he was a just and righteous man, blameless in his [evil] generation; Noah walked [in habitual fellowship] with God… The earth was depraved and putrid in God's sight, and the land was filled with violence (desecration, outrage, assault, and lust for power). And God looked upon the world and saw how degenerate, debase and vicious it was, for all humanity had corrupted their way upon the earth and lost their true direction… (Gen. 6:5-12 Amp).

"God told Noah to make an ark of gopher and cypress wood with rooms (stalls, pens, coops, nests, cages, and compartments), and cover it inside and out with pitch (bitumen). The length shall be 300 cubits', its breadth 50 cubits and its height 30 cubits [that is, 450 ft. x 75 ft. x 45 ft.] … God established his covenant with Noah. He directed Noah to take his sons, their wives and his wife into the ark. Also, to take every living thing, bring two of every sort into the ark, to keep them alive with you; they shall be male and female. The clean animals were for offering acceptable sacrifices to God following the flood. Noah did all that God commanded. God closed the door and the rains came for 40 days and nights and the fountains of the deep poured forth water. The water covered even the highest hills for five months. God set a rainbow in the sky as a reminder of the covenant to never again destroy the world with a flood."[9]

"The total volume of Noah's Ark was roughly 1.5 million cubic feet, which is equal to the total capacity of more than 570 standard stock cars used on a typical railroad. The floor space would be about 100,000 sq. ft. It would hold the equivalent of all the animals in six of our nation's largest cities. Perhaps the animals were all very young and therefore small and would sleep a lot. The ark was designed to withstand the tallest of ocean waves."[10]

Days of Wickedness

Will there ever be a time when this world is as wicked as in Noah's day? Jesus said, "As it was in the days of Noah so it will be at the coming of the Son of Man. For in the days before the flood, people were eating and drinking, marrying and giving in marriage, up to the day Noah entered the ark; and they knew nothing about what would happen until the flood came and took them. That is how it will be at the coming of the Son of Man" (Matt. 24:37-39).

Jesus in speaking to the generation preceding Christ's return, says: "When the Son of Man comes, will he find faith on earth?" (Luke 18:8) Observe the rapidity of social and cultural trends hostile to Christ and his church today: "There will be terrible times in the last days. People will be lovers of themselves, lovers of money, boastful, proud, abusive, disobedient to their parents, ungrateful, unholy, without love, unforgiving, slanderous, without self-control, brutal, not lovers of good, treacherous, rash, conceited, lovers of pleasure rather than lovers of God - having a form of godliness but denying its power. Have nothing to do with them" (II Tim. 3:1-5).

Paul writes, "You know what is holding this wicked one back until it is time for him to come. His mysterious power is already at

[9] The preceding was adapted from the Amplified Bible, Genesis 6-9.

[10] Adapted from the internet.

work, but someone is holding him back. And the wicked one won't appear until that someone is out of the way. Then he will appear but the Lord Jesus will kill him simply by breathing on him. He will be completely destroyed by the Lord's glorious return. When the wicked one appears, Satan will pretend to work all kinds of miracles, wonders, and signs. Lost people will be fooled by his evil deeds. They could be saved but they will refuse to love the truth and accept it. So, God will make sure that they are fooled into believing a lie. All of them will be punished, because they would rather do evil than believe the truth" (II Thess. 2:6-12 CEV). In light of these Scriptures and the trends of hostility toward Jesus and his church, it is clear that before the return of our Lord the world will be similar to Noah's time.

"If God did not spare angels when they sinned, but sent them to hell; ... if he did not spare the ancient world when he brought the flood on its ungodly people; ... if he condemned the cities of Sodom and Gomorrah burning them to ashes, and made them an example of what is going to happen to the ungodly; ... if this is so then the Lord knows how to rescue Godly men from trials and to hold the unrighteous for the day of judgment, while continuing their punishment. This is especially true of those who follow the corrupt desire of the sinful nature and despise authority" (II Pet. 2:4-10).

Today the evils of Noah's day are turned in to entertainment. The proceeds of human trafficking are now larger than the world's drug market. Homosexuality is legalized in fourteen countries - Argentina, Belgium, Canada, Denmark, Iceland, Netherlands, Norway, Portugal, Spain, South Africa, Sweden, New Zealand, Uruguay, and France.

The arms build-up is another of many other indications of our world being filled with violence. "Russia is believed to have 4,300 nuclear weapons, followed by the US with 4,000. There are 9,400 nuclear weapons in military arsenals, with another 5,600-awaiting dismantlement. Nearly 4,000 nuclear weapons are operationally available; 1,800 are ready for use on short notice. The largest Russian bomb, if dropped on New York City, would kill 7.6 million people."[11]

What did Noah do? Noah persevered.

---

[11] Jim Denison's blog, May 25, 2018.

Imagine working many years constructing an ark? Noah had never experienced a rain drop. Water came up from the earth like dew which meant there could be no rainbow. After the flood God put a rainbow in the sky as a promise he would never again destroy the world with a flood. (Gen. 9:12-17). Noah had no idea what a boat was or how to build one. He was busy expanding his estate. Noah was surrounded with degenerate, debase and vicious people; violence was running rampant. The people had no purpose or direction! Noah was different, he stood alone for what was right in the midst of all the wickedness and godlessness. Noah found grace in God's eyes. (Gen. 6:9). When speaking of Noah's time Jesus said: "They did not know or understand until the flood came and swept them all away, so will it be at the coming of the Son of man" (Matt. 24:39 Amp).

For several decades the people observed Noah and his project. I expect many of them were employed by Noah to help with this mammoth "boat." They had to ask questions. I'm sure Noah told them repeatedly why he was giving all his energy to this task. "If we deliberately keep on sinning after we have received the knowledge of the truth, no sacrifice for sins is left, but only a fearful expectation of judgment and of raging fire that will consume the enemies of God" (Heb. 10:26-27). Jesus also said to the Pharisees, "These people's hearts have become calloused" (Matt. 13:15). They deliberately closed their minds to the truth. Today, especially since the Bible is available in our vernacular and since there are hundreds of Christian radio stations and scores of Christian TV stations as well as churches most everywhere, we have no excuse.

Paul says, "God shows his anger from heaven against all sinful', wicked people who suppress the truth by their wickedness. They know the truth about God because he has made it obvious to them. For ever since the world was created, people have seen the earth and sky. Through everything God made, they can clearly see his invisible qualities—his eternal power and divine nature. So, they have no excuse for not knowing God" (Rom. 1:18-20 NLT).

Noah Stood Alone

Noah stood alone. There will come a time when you need to stand alone. Not only did Noah stand-alone - he stood alone for 120 years. What perseverance! Since he was the only God-fearing man, he was forced to listen to the foul language and see wickedness from the hundreds who he had on his payroll in building the ark. Even those in your own family may turn against you. Jesus said, "Brother will betray brother to death, and the father his child, and children will take a stand against their parents, and will have them put to death; You will be hated by all for My name's sake. But he who perseveres and endures to the end will be saved [from spiritual disease and death in the world to come]." (Matt. 10:21-22 Amp).

It's amazing what God can do with one person who is willing to stand alone for him. "Run to and fro through the streets of Jerusalem and see now and take notice! Seek in her broad squares to see if you can find a man [as Abraham sought in Sodom], one who does justice, who seeks truth, sincerity and faithfulness; and I will pardon Jerusalem - for one uncompromisingly righteous person." (Jer. 5:1 Amp). Later God looked for a person to stand in the gap so he would not have to destroy the land. "I looked for a man among them who would build up the wall and stand before me in the gap on behalf of the land so I would not have to destroy it, but I found none. So, I will pour out my wrath on them and consume them with my fiery anger, bringing down on their own heads all they have done, declares the Sovereign Lord" (Ezekiel 22:30-31).

Thousands today must stand alone as they live in hostile, radical jihad territories. (See www.opendoors.org). If you want to grow in your faith read the *Foxes Book of Martyrs* or the *Martyr's Mirror* with 4000 individual accounts of those who martyred for Christ. It's believed that for every martyr there were thirty persons who came to faith in Christ.

Ron stood alone. At noon in the factory where Ron worked when he ate lunch with the men their conversation became more wholesome. When Eugene chose a bowling league of secular men, he had a positive effect on many of those men. When Scott chose to join an international bridgebuilding team, he chose a secular organization and has left a Christian witness to countless persons in several countries.

Daniel persevered as he resolved to not defile himself by eating what the King asked. He made up his mind, determined in his heart, to eat and drink only what God had approved. (Dan. 1:8). Job persevered through all his suffering and finished well. Many do not finish well. Noah, after living faithfully for 120 years, got drunk. (Gen. 9:21). Samson and King David stumbled because of sexual immorality. Absalom fell because of pride and abuse of power. Eli would not discipline his sons and brought disgrace on his family and the nation of Israel. You will make a difference for God if you are willing to stand alone and finish well.

Finish Well

We can finish well: "I am confident of this that he who began a good work in you will carry it on to completion until the day of Christ Jesus" (Phil. 1:6). "Jesus Christ will keep you strong to the end, so that you will be blameless on the day of our Lord Jesus Christ. God, who has called you into fellowship with his son Jesus Christ, our Lord, is faithful" (I Cor. 1:8-9). David writes, "My heart is set on keeping your decrees to the very end" (Ps. 119:112). Paul prays that the Colossian Church will have great endurance and patience. (Col. 1:11). These trials are necessary for us to develop endurance and strength of character. (Rom. 5:3).

After Paul suffered many years for the Lord, his final words of admonition were for us as men and women of God to... "pursue righteousness, godliness, faith, love, endurance (perseverance) and gentleness. Fight the good fight of faith. Take hold of the eternal life to which you were called when you made your good confession in the presence of many witnesses" (I Tim. 6:11-12). Paul told Titus to instruct the older men to develop their endurance. (Titus 2:2). One of the fruits of the Spirit is patience, endurance or perseverance.

When no one is watching you and encouraging you, remember God sees every move you make. Claim God's grace. Without his grace we will give up as we experience everyday life with its trivial and often boring routine. It's important to surround yourself with others who can encourage you. Their examples will booster your spirit to persevere through difficulties. Learn to persevere, even when your work cannot be seen by others.

The word "learn" is very important. We will learn to persevere over time, learning is a process. Jesus learned obedience. Keep your eyes on Jesus and drudgery will not discourage you. Never allow yourself to think that some tasks are beneath your dignity or too insignificant for you to do. Jesus washed the disciple's feet.

Paul praises the Thessalonians, "Among God's churches we boast about your perseverance and faith in all the persecutions and trials you are enduring" (II Thess. 1:4). "We rejoice in our sufferings because suffering produces perseverance; perseverance character...." (Ro. 5:3-4). Peter writes that we are to add perseverance to our faith so we will be productive and effective. (II Pet. 1:6-8). James says the testing of our faith develops perseverance resulting in maturity. (James 1:3-4). Jesus commends the churches of Ephesus and Thyatira for their perseverance. (Rev. 2:2 and 19).

"Since we are surrounded by such a great cloud of witnesses, let us throw off everything that hinders and the sin that so easily entangles, and let us run with perseverance the race marked out for us. Let us fix our eyes on Jesus, the author and perfecter of our faith, who for the joy set before him endured the cross, scorning its shame, and sat down at the right hand of the throne of God. Consider him who endured such opposition from sinful men, so that you will not grow weary and lose heart" (Heb. 12:1-3). Fix your eyes on Jesus. He has blazed the trail and finished well. He's our model. He will mold and shape you. Go with him. He finished well.

Instant Gratification

The call to persevere flies in the face of our culture which demands instant gratification. Christians who are not learning perseverance are continually frustrated, asking why and demanding for God to give them answers. Learn to let God be the time keeper.

Get rid of any excess baggage. Throw off all sin that would hinder your relationship with Jesus and others. If anything comes to mind when you ask God to show you what grieves his Spirit, don't excuse it or argue about it. Confess it and let Jesus wash it away with his cleansing blood. He paid the price. Go free, persevere and get back in the race.

There is a specific race marked out for you. No one else has an identical track. If you aren't faithful, you are hindering the work of God. Persevere, pace yourself. Don't run ahead of God or lag behind. He's developing your character and that takes time. His grace is sufficient for today. When tomorrow comes he will provide the grace and strength you need. Corrie ten Boon was fearful when she knew she was headed for the death camps for hiding Jews during W.W. II. Her godly father told her God's grace will be with you one day at a time. Live in his grace.

"Don't allow yourself to get fatigued doing good. At the right time we will harvest a good crop if we don't give up or quit" (Gal. 6:9 Msg.). "Be firm (steadfast), immovable, always abounding in the work of the Lord - that is, always being superior (excelling, doing more than enough) in the service of the Lord, knowing and being continually aware that your labor in the Lord is not futile—never wasted or to no purpose." (I Cor. 15:58 Amp).

Live into Hebrew 12:1-3, and you will persevere, you will not lose heart but be faithful to the end, then you will hear Jesus' words: "Well done, good and faithful servant." Joy comes in the morning. Jesus looked ahead to eternity. We anticipate by faith the eternal reward that is not worth comparing with the trials we now experience. Every dream, if it is of God will be fulfilled. Be faithful, do your part. Trust God to bring it to pass.

Little Faith and Great Faith

Jesus frequently talked to the disciples about little faith or great faith. Jesus says, since God takes care of the birds and clothes the flowers, will he not much more clothe you, O you of little faith. (Matt. 6:30). Without warning a furious storm came up on the lake while the disciples were in the boat. Jesus was asleep. They woke him saying, "Lord save us! We're going to drown!" Jesus rebuked the storm saying, "Why are you afraid? You have so little faith!" (Matt. 8:26). When Peter saw Jesus walking on the water at Jesus invitation he stepped out of the boat to walk on the water but soon began to sink. He cried out for Jesus to save him. Jesus said, "You of little faith, why did you doubt?" (Matt. 14:31). The disciples asked Jesus why they couldn't heal the demon possessed boy. Jesus said, "Because you have so little faith. I tell you the truth, if you have faith as small as a mustard seed, you can say to this mountain, 'Move from here to there' and it will move. Nothing will be impossible for you" (Matt. 17:20-21). Jesus rebuked the disciples for not believing in his resurrection. (Mark 16:14).

A Roman officer came to Jesus and asked him to heal his servant. The officer told Jesus he was not worthy to have Jesus come to his house but that he should just say the word and his servant would be healed. What great faith! (Luke 7:1-10). A Canaanite Woman came to Jesus requesting he heal her daughter. The woman was put off but persisted. Jesus said, "Woman you have great faith! Your request is granted" (Matt 15:28).

How do we move from little faith to greater faith? There is a clear connection to living in God's word and growing in faith. "Let your roots grow down into him and draw up nourishment from him, so you will grow in faith, strong and vigorous in the truth you were taught. Let your lives overflow with thanksgiving for all he has done" (Col. 2:7 NLT). "Faith comes from listening to this message of good news—the Good News about Christ (Rom 10:17 NLT). "Let the word of Christ, in all their richness, live in our hearts and make you wise" (Col. 3:16 NLT). Jesus says, "If you remain in me and my words remain in you, ask whatever you wish and it will be given you. This is to my Father's glory that you bear much fruit showing yourselves to be my disciples. (John 15:7-8). Faith comes from the hope that is stored for us in heaven. (Col. 1:5).

Walk with Jesus. Observe his responses. We grow in faith knowing we are not alone. "Since we are surrounded by such a great cloud of witnesses, let us throw off everything that hinder and the sin that so easily entangles, and let us run with perseverance the race marked out for us. Let us fix our eyes on Jesus.... Who for the joy set before him, endured the cross, scorning its shame, and sat down at the right hand .... of God. Consider him who endured such opposition from sinful men so that you will not grow weary and lose heart." (Heb. 12:1-3).

Faith is built by associating with those who exhibit a strong faith. Faith is like a muscle, exercise it and it will grow stronger. Peter informs us how to exercise our muscle of faith: "make every effort to add to our faith goodness, knowledge, self-control, perseverance, godliness, brotherly kindness and love. For if you possess these qualities in increasing measure, they will keep you from being ineffective and unproductive in your knowledge of our Lord Jesus Christ. But if anyone does not have them, he is nearsighted and blind, and has forgotten that he has been cleansed from his past sins.... If you do these things, you will never fall, and you will receive a rich welcome into the eternal kingdom of our Lord and Savior Jesus Christ" (II Peter 1:10 -11).

Faith and Worry / Anxiety

Faith and worry are opposites. Worry is negative meditation. Someone said, "Worry is like a rocking chair, it gives you something to do but does not get you anywhere." Faith is positive thinking, positive meditation; meditation that draws its life from the Living Word. Faith is spelled T-R-U-S-T. We too often spell it R-I-S-K. Doing the same things over and over expecting to get different results is not faith. We get stuck in our ways. The Holy Spirit wants to teach us new approaches. He will surprise you as you trust him. Take that step of faith!

After Jesus fed the 5,000, the people were searching for him. When they found him, he said they were following him because he fed them. He continued, "Do not work for food that spoils, but for food that endures to eternal life... Then they asked him, 'What must we do to do the works God requires?' Jesus answered, 'the work of God is to believe (put your faith, i.e. trust in, cling to and rely upon) in the one he has sent'" (John 6:26-29).

As Paul comes to the end of his life he says, "Fight the good fight of faith." (I Tim. 6:12). The only battle or fight you have is, "do I believe—do I have faith in Jesus, his atonement and resurrection."

Our faith (or belief) is based in Jesus Christ and his atonement. This faith leads to doing good works. "Faith by itself, if it is not accompanied by action, is dead.... Do not merely listen to the word, and so deceive yourselves. Do what it says" (James 1:17, 22). Paul concludes his letter to the Romans; "this message is made known to all Gentiles so that they might believe (have faith) and obey Christ" (16:27 NLT). "Do not be anxious about anything, but in everything, by prayers and petition, with thanksgiving, present your requests to God. And the peace of God... will guard your hearts and minds in Christ Jesus" (Phil. 4:6-7).

ABRAHAM

Father of the Faithful

HEB. 11:8 -19 & GEN.12:1-25:18

"By faith Abraham, when called to go to a place he would later receive as his possession, obeyed and went, even though he did not know where he was going. By faith he made his home in the promised land like a stranger in a foreign country; he lived in tents, as did Isaac and Jacob, who are heirs with him of the same promise. For he was looking forward to the city with foundations, whose architect and builder is God. By faith Abraham, even though he was past age - and Sarah herself was barren - was enabled to become a father because he considered him faithful who had made the promise. And so, from this one man, and he as good as dead, came descendants as numerous as the stars in the sky and as countless as the sand on the seashore...." (Heb. 11:8-12).

Abraham occupies nearly half the space in our "Faith Chapter." Everyone in God's Hall of Faith (Heb. 11), except Abel and Enoch, who were born before Abraham, is a descendant of Abraham. (Abraham is recognized in seven other books of the Bible.)

"The Lord had said to Abram, 'Leave your native country, your relatives, and your father's family, and go to the land that I will show you. I will make you into a great nation. I will bless you and make you famous, and you will be a blessing to others. I will bless those who bless you and curse those who treat you with contempt. All the families on earth will be blessed through you. So, Abraham departed.'" (Gen. 12:1-4 NLT).

Ur, where Abraham lived, was a wealthy country with many opulent houses. However, it was a city of wickedness, a cesspool of iniquity and human sacrifice. When God instructed Abram (his name was later changed to Abraham, Gen. 17:5) to move he departed immediately taking his wife, father and his nephew, Lot, and his servants.

Delaying God's Instructions Is Disobedience

When God called, Abram responded immediately. (Gen. 12:1-4). When God warned Joseph, he got up in the middle of the night to take Mary and Jesus to Egypt. (Matt. 2:13-14). Delayed obedience is not obedience. If you ask your child to clean their room today and they say, "I will do it tomorrow" that is disobedience. How often have you sensed God asking you to encourage someone? Don't keep putting it off. Begin to prepare immediately. If you delay you will find the joy of the Lord and the power of the resurrection lacking. Fear will take the place of implementation. Obey God immediately. Checking with other Christians is often appropriate but be careful or they will give you a dozen reasons why you need to delay. Many of our unsaved friends put off responding to Jesus' invitation to trust in him for eternal life. We are not promised our next breath. Persistently disobeying the Holy Spirit hardens our hearts so we cannot hear his voice.

The Eternal Focus

Abram, in addition to accepting the promise that his descendants would inherit the land, looked forward to eternity, "for he was looking forward to the city with foundations, whose architect and builder is God" (Heb. 11:10-11). Do you live with a consciousness of eternity? Abraham had a long-range view. Many people focus only on this life. "What is your life? You are a mist that appears for a little while and then vanishes" (James 4:14). "Don't boast about tomorrow, for you do not know what a day may bring forth" (Prov. 27:1). "My life is but a breath" (Job 7:7). Since our short span of life is so minuscule compared to eternity we should be impelled to live as fully committed disciples of Christ.

We are on probation. How we live today will determine our future destiny for billions of years and beyond. There will be a time of Reckoning. Don't live thoughtlessly, consider the brevity of life compared to the length of eternity. Jesus said, "I tell you that men will have to give account on the Day of Judgment for every careless word they have spoken. For by your words you will be acquitted, and by your words you will be condemned" (Matt. 12:36-37).

More than three hundred times we are reminded of Jesus' return. Our blessed hope is the coming of the Lord. (Titus 2:13). From prison, Paul writes that his citizenship is in heaven and he eagerly awaited Jesus' return. (Phil. 3:20). The New Testament Christians anxiously anticipated the Lord's return. Having our focus on Jesus' return will help us live a pure and fruitful life. (I John 3:3). A few verses before our faith chapter, (Heb. 10:35) the Christians "sympathized with those in prison and joyfully accepted the confiscation of their property, because they knew that they had a better and lasting possession." These Christians joyfully accepted the fact their possessions were taken because their focus was on a far better country.

Abraham Stumbles

A famine occurred, so Abram moved temporarily to Egypt (12:10). When he entered Egypt he asked Sarai, his unusually beautiful wife, to identify herself as his sister because he believed the men would kill him, so they could have Sarai. God covered Abraham and kept him safe, even though He could have punished him for his doubt in God's ability to keep both him and Sarai safe from Pharaoh and his men. Pharaoh sent Abram many gifts and took Sarai into his haram. God sent a plague to Pharaoh's household because he took Sarai. When Pharaoh realized what he had done, he escorted Abram and his household out of the country.

Did Abram lie? Rahab hid two spies Joshua had sent. When the king's messengers who were searching for them arrived she told them she did not know where they came from. (Joshua 2:2-7). Samuel was afraid to anoint David as king of Israel because he was afraid Saul would kill him. God told Samuel to tell everyone that he came to offer a sacrifice to the Lord. Under this cover he was able to anoint David as the new king of Israel. (I Samuel 16:2-13).

The New Testament Scriptures throw light on this subject: "In God's divine forbearance He had passed over and ignored former sins without punishment." (Rom. 3:25b). "Such [former] ages of ignorance God ignored and allowed to pass unnoticed; but now He charges all people everywhere to repent - [that is], to change their minds for the better and heartily to amend their ways, with abhorrence for their past sins." (Acts 17:30 Amp).

God condemns lying and praises those who deal truthfully. But he who keeps some knowledge to himself is wise. "A prudent man is reluctant to display his knowledge, the heart of (self-confident) fools proclaims their folly" (Proverbs 12:23). There are times it can be foolish to tell everything you know. When Menno Simons, the priest turned from the Catholic Church, became an outlaw by joining the Anabaptists, the authorities were searching for his life. He was driving a team of horses pulling a wagon. The authorities stopped him to ask if Menno was in his wagon. He turned around, looked and said, I don't see him. His life was spared. Jesus did not answer everything people asked Him. There was never any deceit in Jesus. (Isaiah 53:9).

Greed Entered Nephew Lot

When the king of Egypt realized that God was punishing him because he had taken Sarai, he sent them away. They and their household moved to Judah. (Gen. 13:1). Abram was rich with many servants and much cattle. Lot, his nephew, was also blessed with an abundance of livestock. The land could not support both Abraham and Lot's cattle occupying the same pasture, so Abram proposed to his nephew that he choose to take the land either to his left or right and that he would take whichever Lot did not choose. Lot chose the more productive fields in the Jordan Valley near Sodom. Lot knew better. He was too immature to live close to the wickedness of Sodom. There are times when we need to recognize that we are not strong enough to settle next door to temptation.

Abraham left Lot learn for himself. I feel sure Abram warned Lot of God's displeasure with the wickedness of Sodom. Lot was blinded by the choice of the better pasture - a better business deal. Lot suffered for this poor choice and even lost his wife whose heart was on her possessions. (Gen. 19:26). "Do not love the world or anything in the world. If anyone loves the world, the love of the Father is not in him. For everything in the world—the cravings of sinful man, the lust of his eyes and the boasting of what he has and does—comes not from the Father but from the world. The world and its desires pass away, but the man who does the will of God lives forever" (I John 2:15-17). Lot and his wife surrendered to the "lust of the eye."

Today the "lust of the eye" causes masses of Christians to run up charge card debt making life miserable for everyone. If we can't manage our finances, we are not managing our life. "Americans spend $143,280 to 'treat themselves' in a lifetime... According to the study, the average American spends $199 a month, or about 22 percent of their disposable income, on non-essentials for themselves — including both traditional "self-care" treats and restorative or luxury experiences... Middle income families spend 50 percent on luxuries and 50 percent on necessities... Fifty-six percent of those surveyed admitted they crave a more luxurious lifestyle than they currently have. In the biblical narrative, money is a gift and the love of money is a trap (1 Tim. 6:10 & Deut. 10:14). The generosity of Theophilus funded the work of Dr. Luke and the contentment of Lydia advanced the kingdom eventually into Europe (Luke 1:1-4 & Acts 16:11-40). Don't be afraid to treat yourself, just don't get consumed in yourself."[12]

Can you imagine if Christians would eliminate one half of their luxury goods, they could afford to give far more than a tithe to God's work. Self-gratification people never consider giving the Lord his due. They think they must have whatever their heart desires and have it now. Paul tells Timothy, "Be satisfied just to have food and clothes" (I Tim. 6:8).

Jesus spoke more about riches than any other subject. Jesus says, in the parable of the sower, the thorny ground represents those who hear and accept the Good News, but all too quickly the message is crowded out by the cares of this life and the lure of wealth, so no crop is produced." (Matt. 13:22 NLT). Again, he says, "No one can serve two masters. Either he will have the one and love the other, or he will be devoted to the one and despise the other. You cannot serve

---

12 Nick Pitts, Executive Director of The Institute of Global Engagement in his Daily Briefings, July 7, 2018.

both God and Money" (Matt. 6:24). The deceitfulness of riches chokes out God's Word. (Matt. 13:22).

"The love of money is at the root of all kinds of evil. And some people, craving money, have wandered from the faith and pierced themselves with many sorrows... Tell those who are rich in this world not to put their trust in riches which will soon be gone." (I Tim. 6:10, 17 NLT). When the stock market plunges, the hospital emergency rooms are inundated and the suicide rate soars. Is your heart on God's Kingdom or on acquiring more things?

Rescue Those Who Are Straying

Sodom was at war. (Gen. 14). The enemy captured Lot and his household. Even though Lot made a wrong choice and wandered from God, Uncle Abraham came to Lot's rescue. God wants us to rescue people. In most churches when someone starts missing church no one pays attention. Do we pray for them? Do we have enough compassion to be assertive and say, "We've been missing you, or we missed you the last couple Sundays? Is everything ok?" If you have a good relationship with them you can soon tell if they have a good reason of if they are drifting away. "If someone among you wanders away from the truth and is brought back, you can be sure that whoever brings the sinner back will save that person from death and bring about the forgiveness of many sins." (James 5:19-20 NLT). Jesus reminds us that if a sheep goes astray we are to do all we can to restore it. (Luke 15:4-7). "If another believer sins, rebuke that person; then if there is repentance forgive. Even if that person wrongs you seven times a day and each time turns again and asks forgiveness, you must forgive" (Luke 17:3-4 NLT).

Tithes

In Chapter 14:18-20 Abraham introduces the principle of giving tithes. Lot was captured. Abraham defeated Lot's captors. In response Abraham gave a tenth of all the spoils to Melchizedek. Melchizedek is a type of Christ. Today less than ten percent of Christians tithe. The tithe is not a legal requirement. If God required tithes under the Old Testament law what does he expect from us who live under the blessing of the covenant of grace in the New Testament? (II Cor. 3:7-18). Everything we have belongs to him. As Paul writes: "What do you have that you have not received" (I Cor. 4:7). Christians spend more for junk food or pet food than we give to the Kingdom of God. Many give more to the restaurant owner Sunday noon than they give in the Sunday morning offering. They are better tippers than tithers. "If you have enough money to live well, and see a brother or sister in need and refuse to help - how can God's love be in that person?" (I John 3:17 NLT). The poor and needy are all around us if we have hearts and eyes to see them.[13]

I expect all who read this book are rich when we consider that less than half the people of the world have never talked on a phone. They live on $2.50 a day. One fourth of India's population, that's more than the population of the U.S. live on less than $1.25 a day. To own a bicycle in many countries you are considered rich.

The Pain of Childlessness

For most of their lives Abram and Sarah had no children. How could the promises of many nations come from Abram if he had no children? Abram suggested that his chief servant, Eliezer, be made his heir, but God said, "This man will not be your heir" (Gen. 15:1-4). Sarah steps in taking God's role to try to find a way to fulfill God's promise. She suggested to Abram that he sleep with Hagar, a slave brought back from Egypt, so he could have a child. Abram, unwisely agreed. He was delighted when Ishmael was born, but this was not God's plan.

A history of great pain and suffering which we are still feeling today resulted from their decision to have a child by Hagar. The Jews and Arabs were not always fighting each other. In Acts 2, Arabic was one of the languages spoken on Pentecost. Paul spent three years in the Arabian desert. Historians state that Arab Christianity has been around since the beginning of the formation of the church. God will bring the nations together. (60:1-7). As Christians we need to bring our biases to the cross and beg for God to give us new glasses to see the peace he intends for Jews and Arabs and for all nations. God

---

13 For additional information on "tithes" see the chapter on Malachi.

loves both Isaac's and Ishmael's children. Do all you can to remove the walls that divide us and stop the needless bloodshed.

There are more Arabs coming to Christ today than any time in history. "There were only five movements of Muslims to Christianity prior to the 20th century. But in just the first 12 years of the 21st century, we can document 69 movements of Muslims to faith and baptism in Christ Jesus. Several of these contemporary movements number in the tens of thousands."[14]

Polygamy

Polygamy was never God's best plan for humankind. In Matthew 5 Jesus said five times, "you have heard it said, but I say to you." Jesus introduces a higher standard than polygamy. (Matt. 5:27-32). God permitted polygamy because of the hardness of the hearts of the people. (Matt. 19:8). There are no truly happy and fulfilled marriages outside of one man and one woman. Jealousy always raises its ugly head. God's design for marriage was monogamy from the beginning. "A man shall leave his father and mother and be joined to his wife, and the two shall become one flesh" (Matt. 19:4–5). Paul likewise made clear what God's ideal for marriage is: "Let each man have his own wife, and let each woman have her own husband" (1 Cor. 7:2). Disobedience to that standard has always resulted in evil consequences. David's polygamous heart led to his sin with Bathsheba. Solomon's marital philandering destroyed him and divided his kingdom (1 Kings 11:4). No good has ever come from any violation of the "one-flesh" principle of monogamy.

God made a covenant with Abram. (Gen. 17). He changed his name from Abram (exalted father) to Abraham (the father of many nations). Abraham's part in this covenant was to see that all the males eight days and older had to be circumcised. (17:9:14). This of course involved pain. One of the principles of the Christian faith is that God provides salvation and blessing after blessing, but he usually tests us with some painful things that are hard for us to let go. Be prepared and expect this so you are not caught by surprise. (Heb. 12:6). God loves

---

14 www.PreierChristianity.com. June 2016, Muslims Turning to Christ—A Global Phenomena.

you and knows you will not learn to fly, unless you are pushed out of your comfortable nest, like eaglets taking their first flight.

There is no gain without pain. There is no growth without opposition. Paul writes, "We sent Timothy...to strengthen and encourage you in your faith, so that no one would be unsettled by these trials. You know that we were destined for them. When we were with you, we kept telling you that we would be persecuted" (I Thess. 3:2-4). Jesus said, "All men will hate you because of me" (Mark 13:13). "Everyone who wants to live a godly life will be persecuted" (II Tim. 3:12).

Nothing Is Impossible with God

Nothing is impossible with God. Thirteen years went by. God promised Abraham if he would be faithful he would bless him with as many descendants as the stars of the universe. (Gen. 17:19). Impossible? He was 99 and Sarah was 90. The Lord appeared to them in the form of three men who informed them that God would bless them with a son, Isaac. Isaac was to be the chosen son whose posterity would bring the Messiah into the world. (Ch. 18).

Being past age to have children, they believed God would fulfill his promise. (Heb. 11:11-12). Of Abraham it was said, "He did not waver through unbelief regarding the promise of God but was strengthened in his faith and gave glory to God, being fully persuaded that God had power to do what he had promised. This is why it was credited to him as righteousness. The words 'it was credited to him' were written not for him alone, but also for us, to whom God will credit righteousness—for us who believe in him who raised Jesus from the dead. He was delivered over to death for our sins and was raised to life for our justification" (Ro. 4:20-24). Just as Abraham was justified by faith we are justified by placing our faith in Jesus' death and resurrection.

Supreme Test

The supreme test was yet to come. When Isaac had reached his early teens, God said to Abraham, "Take your son, your only son Isaac, whom you love, and go to the region of Moriah and offer him there as a burnt offering upon one of the mountains of which I will tell you." (Gen. 22:2). Even though Abraham had been accustomed to human sacrifices in his pagan life in Ur, how could this command possibly fit into the plan of God? But Abraham amazingly left early the next morning in obedience to God's plan.

God has given you a vision of what you are to do. Think of yourself according to the measure of faith God has given you. (Rom. 12:3 - 8). Like Abraham, God often allows our vision to be obliterated from our spiritual eyes. He does this to get our eyes off the vision and upon him because the vision can so easily become more important than our relationship with God. You must come to the place where you say: "Lord I don't understand what is happening but I will love and serve you even if the vision is never fulfilled." Job said, "Though he slay me yet will I serve him." Don't let your vision become your idol. This happens when our focus is on our vision instead of on the source of the vision. The question; do you love God more than your vision?

Abraham began the journey taking two servants, his son Isaac, and wood for the offering. On the third day, they drew near to the place of sacrifice. When Isaac asked the searching question, "Behold, the fire and the wood: but where is the lamb for the burnt offering?" Abraham replied, "God will provide for Himself the lamb for the burnt offering, my son" (Gen. 22:7-8).

When they came to the place, Abraham apparently had to tell Isaac what he was about to do. And Isaac, being a strong young man, had to be willing to be bound on the altar as God had directed Abraham. Just as Abraham took the knife to take the life of his own son, God stayed his hand, and told him to offer instead, a ram caught in a nearby thicket. Hebrews 11:17-19: "By faith when God tested him, he offered Isaac as a sacrifice. He who had received the promises was about to sacrifice his one and only son, even though God had said to him, 'It is through Isaac that your offspring will be reckoned.' Abraham reasoned that God could raise the dead, and figuratively speaking, he did receive Isaac back from death.'" Abraham believed if God commanded him to sacrifice what was most valuable to him that God would raise Isaac from death to fulfill the promise of his seed bringing the Messiah.

God's Ultimate Sacrifice

God intervened and saved the life of Isaac; however, God did not intervene when his own Son hung on the cross and cried, "My, God why have you forsaken me?" There was no other acceptable sacrifice for our sins. Thank God for Jesus remaining on the cross to redeem us from our sin. As Abraham trusted God to overcome any obstacle to fulfill God's covenant we too must put our faith in Jesus who God raised from death. "God promised through the prophets... regarding his Son, who as to his human nature was a descendant of David, and who through the Spirt of holiness was declared with power to be the Son of God by his resurrection from the death: Jesus Christ our Lord" (Ro. 1:2-4).

God intervened to save Isaac's life. There are many times God intervenes to save us from harm and death, however other times we must trust him even though he allows us to take the path of suffering and martyrdom. James was martyred, but Peter walks out of prison the next morning a free man. (Acts 12). On the other hand, Paul knew he was to come to Rome, but after fourteen days without food and water, the 276 men on board the ship to Rome felt sure the ship was breaking up and gave up all hope, but God appeared and rescued everyone. (Acts. 27-28). We are not promised deliverance from pain and suffering, but we are promised he will never forsake us. The disciples died a martyr's death. Look at the miracle of the church which is stronger than ever after two thousand years of opposition. More than one hundred thousand are baptized in Christ every day.

When Jesus was asked, "What must we do to do the works God requires?" Jesus answered, "This is the work (service) that God asks of you, that you believe in the One Whom He has sent—that you cleave to, rely on and have faith in His messenger" (John 6:29 Amp.). Abraham believed God and his faith was counted to him as righteousness—a phrase used by Paul and James five times. When we walk by faith, the supernatural becomes natural, i.e. the people we meet, the words we say are directed by the Holy Spirit. What peace and joy that brings.

Abraham is the only person in the Old Testament who is called the friend of God. (Is. 41:8; II Chron. 20:7). Jesus said, "You are my friends if you do what I command" (John 15:14). Is Jesus your friend? If you walk in faith, abiding in Jesus as the branch abides in the vine, you are his friend.

SOME PEOPLE KNOW HIM NOT.

Some know about him
Some know him as Savior
Some know him as Lord
Some know him as Father
Very few know him as a Friend.

Abraham Intercedes for Sodom

Abraham intercedes for Sodom. (Gen. 18:16-33). Abraham asked God if he would take both the righteous and the wicked when he destroys the city of Sodom. He reasoned with God to spare the city if there were fifty righteous. God assured him that he would spare the city for fifty righteous persons if he could find them. Then Abraham bargained with God for forty-five, then forty, then thirty, twenty and ten. God promised he would not destroy the city if he found ten righteous persons there. Might God have spared the city for even one righteous person? (Jer. 5:1, Ezekiel 22:30). Why hasn't God destroyed America? There are still righteous persons among us. Be sure you are one of them. Unless God can find righteous persons, we will be like the Thessalonians who were destined for sufferings. (I Thess. 3:3), and eventually for destruction.

Is Jesus disappointed at your faith level? Give Christians a choice of working ten hours or praying one hour. Few would choose the one hour because prayer takes faith, that's one reason why our prayer meetings are poorly attended and our churches are not impacting our communities. I have ministered in seventy some congregations as a church consultant and frequently asked to come for the prayer time before the worship service. Attendance is usually often only the pastor and two or three others.

When I pray for missionaries, for those who are persecuted, for the refugees, those who are dying of hunger, do I believe my prayers will make a difference? Often the Lord will instruct us to help meet the needs of persons we pray for. Don't let that hinder you. God will give you both wisdom and strength to pray with faith and follow through with appropriate actions. Faith without works is dead. (James 2:14-26).

Let me repeat: God answers every prayer—"yes," "no" or "wait." God answers every prayer for healing—with a physical miracle of healing or even a greater miracle: "my grace is sufficient." When a paraplegic like Joni Erickson Tada testifies of the joy of the Lord, it raises my faith level. God never makes a mistake. "And we know that in all things God works for the good of those who love him, who have been called according to his purpose." (Rom. 8:28 NIV).

Thank God for His Answers

God answers our prayers but too often we forget to thank him or give him credit. We think it's just a coincident. Are we cowards, too shy to say, "God answered my prayer"? When is the last time you shared how God's answered your prayers? We are commanded to tell of his acts which builds faith for us and for others. When Paul had a thorn, God said, "My grace is sufficient for you for my power is made perfect in weakness. Therefore, I will boast all the more gladly about my weaknesses, so that Christ's power may rest on me. That is why... I delight in weaknesses, in insults, in hardships, in persecutions, in difficulties. For when I am weak, then I am strong" (II Cor. 12:9-10). Boast on God!

SARAH

Mother of Nations

HEBREWS 11:11

Sarah and Rahab are the only women mentioned in God's Hall of Fame. Sarah is the half-sister of Abram and also his wife. Her birth name was, Sarai - "my princess." Her name was changed to Sarah as part of God's covenant after Ismael was born. Sarah means a woman of high rank. (Gen. 17:15). Abraham shared God's covenant with Sarah. She is included in God's Hall of Faith because she believed God would keep his promises. (Heb. 11:11).

Sarah carried the burden of childlessness for many years. She longed to see God' promises fulfilled. Her faith was rewarded when she was past child-bearing age and gave birth to Isaac at age 90. Abraham could never become the patriarch of a great nation if Sarah did not first become mother to his offspring.

Women Are Not Second-Class

Peter refers to Sarah in one of the more difficult passages in the New Testament because it flies in the face of our culture. "You wives must accept the authority of your husbands. Then, even if some refuse to obey the Good News, your godly lives will speak to them without any words. They will be won over by observing your pure and reverent lives. Don't be concerned about the outward beauty of fancy hair-styles, expensive jewelry, or beautiful clothes. You should clothe yourselves instead with the beauty that comes from within, the unfading beauty of a gentle and quiet spirit which is so precious to God. This is how the holy women of old made themselves beautiful. They trusted in God and accepted the authority of their husbands. For instance, Sarah obeyed her husband, Abraham, and called him her master. You are her daughters when you do what is right without fear of what your husbands might do. In the same way, you husbands must give honor to your wives. Treat your wife with understanding as you live together. She may be weaker than you are, but she is your equal partner in God's gift of new life. Treat her as you should so your prayers will not be hindered." (I Peter 3:1-7 NLT).

Peter presents a revolutionary concept for that culture. Christian women will be different by how they act and how they respect their husbands. Husbands are to treat their wives as equal partners in God's grace. Women, in the time of Peter, were often considered as property with the husbands having complete authority in the home. They had no public life, no education. When a woman came to faith in Christ without her husband's consent, she was often treated with contempt and even physical abuse. In this situation, the Christian wife was to live an exemplary life in hopes that her unchristian husband would allow her to practice her faith and see her selfless sacrificial love as so attractive that he would come to the Christian faith. Even today there is no more effective witness than a Godly life.

There were thousands of prostitutes serving in the pagan temples. Women who were prostitutes advertised their availability by taking down their hair from the top of their head, decorating it and using it to draw attention to themselves. Many would sling their hair around to be noticed. The temptation was for women to earn their living with the temple worship of the human body.

Submission is being willing to cooperate voluntarily out of love and respect. In truly Christian families submission is mutual. "Submit to one another out of reverence for Christ." (Eph. 5:21). Submission can be a positive witness. Jesus was submissive as he hung on the cross. Being submissive often helps others see Christ in us as we sacrifice time, effort and even pain to go the second mile or extend blessings when we are cursed. Christian submission never requires us to disobey God, remain in an unsafe situation, or participate in what our conscience forbids. One-sided submission requires tremendous strength which only the Holy Spirit can provide.

When Peter referred to the wife as weaker he is not referring to her intellect or her standing before God. (v. 6). He is referring to physical strength. Women were abused, sent from the home for unreasonable reasons, like putting too much salt on the food or simply because she displeases him in any way. This meant they were often left to the abuse of evil men and many even starved to death. In most nations of the world today women do not enjoy the respect God designed women to experience. Christian men are responsible to extend to women respect, honor and blessing in their daily living. In fact, if Christian husbands do not do this God will not hear their prayers. (v. 7). There are so many divorces even among "Christians" because we do not honor and respect our partners.

Beauty Is Not Always an Asset

Beauty was detrimental for Sarah. When famine came, they traveled to Egypt. (Gen. 12:10). Abraham passed Sarah off as his sister to Pharaoh. He believed Pharaoh would kill him so he could add Sarah to his harem. Imagine being Sarah in this situation. Abraham could have trusted God to protect their marriage. (v.12).

God punished the King in Egypt for taking Sarah into his palace. In fear he forced Abraham and Sarah to leave Egypt and return to Bethel. Together, they lived in the land of promise as in a foreign country, dwelling in tents in anticipation of the eternal city whose builder and maker is God. (Heb. 11:9–10).

Wherever Sarah went, she instantly received favor and privilege because of her beauty. Beauty can spoil the best of women tempting them to be proud and arrogant. Today ninety percent of Hollywood stars are not satisfied with their looks. Americans spend billions of dollars trying to imitate these movie stars. Most of them are poor models for our youth to emulate. Their divorcee and suicide rates are far above that of the general population. Those who idolize them become like them. Too often church attenders can name movie stars but cannot name one of the Gospels or one of the twelve disciples.

Inner beauty is what counts for Christian women. That doesn't mean that she should look sloppy or slovenly. Inward beauty, of a gentle and quiet spirit is far more important in our witness for Christ than outward beauty. "I want women to be modest in their appearance. They should wear decent and appropriate clothing and not draw attention to themselves by the way they fix their hair or by wearing gold or pearls or expensive clothes. For women who claim to be devoted to God should make themselves attractive by the good things they do. (I Timothy 2:8-10 NLT).

Our culture has so inundated church life that there is little difference between those who claim to be Christian and those who follow the culture with its worship of fashion. Older women are to teach the younger women. (Titus 2:4). Today many youths have little respect for the older generation. Numerous Christian youths grow up copying the world of fashion and immodesty not realizing and ignoring how this impacts the minds of both men and women. Jesus reminds us that if we are to see God, we must have a pure heart. (Matt. 5:8). We can help each other by not calling attention to ourselves with our attire or lack of attire. Solomon writes: "Charm and grace are deceptive, and beauty is vain [because it is not lasting], but a woman who reverently and worshipfully fears the Lord, she shall be praised!" (Prov. 31:30 Amp).

Today more than half of the married men and women admit to having committed emotional, if not physical adultery. Jesus made it clear that to look upon a woman with lust is the same as adultery. (Matt. 5:28). If you are into pornography as millions are today, know that you will greatly harm both yourself and your marriage. The Lord will bless Christian women today who are overflowing with inward beauty which results in a spirit of quiet confidence which overcomes the sensual fashions of our culture.

Porn—An Epidemic

"Sixty-Eight percent of Christian men view porn on a regular basis."[15] "During World War II, Nazi Germany dropped pornographic pamphlets from the sky over enemy territory. The reason: to distract the soldiers minds with fascinations causing them to ignore the front line. ... Imagine conquering an entire nation in less than sixty years by simply planting a destructive seed in the minds of a few men and watching it spread to the masses. That is what Satan did through the likes of Hugh Heffner and Bob Gaccione in the 50s when Playboy and Penthouse became nationally distributed magazines. Over the years, images of nude women and men engaged in

15 *Christianity Today Magazine*, September 2017, p. 2.

sexual acts have jumped from the pages of embarrassing to purchase magazines to the privacy of our own personal computer screens. Today, US porn revenue exceeds the revenues of ABC, CBS, and NBC combined, and contrary to its previous consumer group of mostly adult males, its largest consumer demographic today is 12–17-year-old males and females. ...

"There are two effective steps to deliverance for the grips of pornography and sexual sin.... Both are absolutely necessary for success: Realize the fullness of your sin and the damage it is doing to you, your family and your church. Admit that you are powerless over a sin that has gripped your life. Make a solemn commitment never to return to it, and immediately distance yourself from anything that enables your use (including late nights alone with your computer or mobile device, inappropriate chat and, if you've gone that far, visits to the wrong side of town). Secondly, find a porn recovery program that works for you. ...

"As you fight the good fight, remember the strategy of porn. Satan doesn't want your fantasy life—he wants your home. Begin a counter assault on your enemy and use every means at your disposal. Refuse to be destroyed. Pastors who address their porn usage with desperate honesty, bravely forging ahead to accountability, can experience the "good" God intends. Going the distance to full recovery and healing can transform the problem into a God-given rebirth of a pastor's heart, health and marriage."[16]

Women in Ministry

Today there is some controversy about women serving in ministry positions in the church. Women and men are equally loved by God, and may be equally called to ministry as Paul says there is neither male or female. (Gal. 3:26-29). Junias was an apostle. (Ro. 16:7). Phoebe was a deaconess. (Ro. 16:1). It appears that Lydia was a leader in the church that met in her home. (Acts 16:14, 40). Philip's four daughters prophesied. (Acts 21:9). Priscilla and her husband Aquila "explained to [Apollos] the way of God more adequately"

[16] These three paragraphs are adapted from Paul S. Kendall, Kendall Family Network Feb. 5, 2018.

(Acts 18:26). And Mary Magdalene was the first one to tell of Jesus's resurrection (John 20:17-18).

Paul commends women like Euodia and Syntyche who he said, "contended at my side in the cause of the gospel" (Phil 4:3). He commends Tryphena, Tryphosa, Mary and Persis as "women who work hard in the Lord" (Ro 16:6, 12). It's clear that women served in the vital role of sharing God's good news with the lost world.

When women prayed or prophesied, they were to cover their heads. (I Cor. 11:4-10). They were to keep their hair up rather than let it hang loose as the prostitutes did. In First Corinthians 14:33-35 and First Timothy 2:9-12 the women were to be silent in the church in Corinth and Ephesis. Why was this? Women in these cities were not permitted to go to school. They had very little biblical instruction. They had not learned what was orderly—some were apparently disrupting the public worship services by inquiring or asking questions about what was being said. They are not to voice these questions interrupting the worship service but to ask their own husbands at home. If this was meant to be universal command it would mean women could not serve in teaching children, teaching each other, or hold any office in the church that involved speaking—even singing would be off limits for them. Therefore, these two passages need to be understood to apply to their local context not to all churches for all time.

Sarah Takes God's Role

Sarah waited ten long childless years after they arrived in Canaan before she asked Abraham to take Hagar as his wife. (Gen. 16:3). She knew since she was seventy-five and postmenopausal hope was gone. Why did God withhold the privilege of childbirth? When Sarah considered her circumstances, she believed she would never have a child, so she decided to give her maid to Abraham to father a child. She believed this was the only way God's promise to Abraham was ever going to be fulfilled. Sarah's natural logic took God's role upon herself to try to find a way for God to fulfill his promise to Abraham.

God's design for marriage was monogamy from the beginning. "A man shall leave his father and mother and be joined to his wife, and the two shall become one flesh" (Matt. 19:4–5). No good has ever come from any violation of the "one-flesh" principle of monogamy.

Living with Guilt

Sarah lived with guilt. As soon as Hagar conceived, Sarah knew it was a grave mistake. Hagar was contentious toward Sarah. Sarah despised her. (Gen. 16:4-6). When Isaac was weaned about age three, Abraham gave a celebration. (21:8). Sarah saw Ishmael making fun of little Isaac. (v. 9). In Sarah's furry she compelled Abraham to remove Hagar and Ishmael even though they had no place to go. Living with that decision had to weigh heavily on Sarah's conscience. She was miserable and made those around her miserable. Some of the tensions we see in the Middle East today are rooted in Sarah's foolhardy tactic to try to concoct a manmade solution to her dilemma. When we do not follow God's way, we do things we never thought we would even consider doing. The way of the transgressor is hard. (Prov. 13:15).

One of the most difficult admonitions in Scripture is: "Do all things without grumbling and faultfinding and complaining [against God] and questioning and doubting [among yourselves]. (Phil. 2:14 Amp). The previous verse shows us how we can live without grumbling and complaining: "God is working in you, giving you the desire to obey him and the power to do what pleases him." (NLT). As you abide in Jesus, his Spirit will enable you to overcome this disgusting habit. Do you complain or do you just vent? Our fallen nature draws us naturally to see the worst in a situation. Venting with a desire to improve the situation is healthy and opens the door of faith as we trust God to give us eyes to see as he sees. Tests and temptations are an opportunity to draw near to God and receive his wisdom.

Despite her sin, Sarah believed God's promise to Abraham that God would provide an heir from their union. (Heb. 11:11). She knew that God wanted to make Abraham the leader of nations. Her belief enabled her to overlook the earthly inconvenience of leaving all her familiar surroundings, sever ties with her family and commit to a life of rootless wandering. The first leg of the journey from Ur to Haran was more than 600 miles. Sarah apparently does not complain but seems quite willing to go with her husband. After Sarah's father-in-law, Terah, died they traveled on foot to Canaan, a journey of seven weeks covering another 350 miles. She models a submitting wife to her husband's leadership. (I Peter 3:6). When they arrived in Canaan, Abraham built an altar which was an anchor for them, since they were nomads for the remainder of their days.

Rootless Americans

Sarah moved frequently. She was in her sixties when she made her first move from their home in Ur. Today the average family moves several times during their lifetime. Taking up our roots and moving to a new community produces emotional stress and too often results in marriages breaking up. Our children may find it difficult to change schools and find new friends at school and church. Sarah made the moves trusting in God and her husband. How many wives like Sarah have learned to trust God wherever he leads? How many Christians are willing to move to care for their aging parents or to help plant a church? Often when Christians move because of a new job they are more concerned about the school than they are about finding a good church. Too often Christian parents are more than satisfied if their kids are "good kids." They don't think about the huge difference between "good kids" compared with "godly kids." Often school activities take priority over church activities. Children soon realize that school and sports are more important than faith in God.

Delayed Gratification

(Also see Jacob for this theme.)

When Ishmael was born to Hagar, Abraham was eighty-six years old. (Gen. 16:16). For thirteen more frustrating years Sarah remained barren. By that time, she was eighty-nine. She had lived in Canaan for twenty-four years. Her husband was about to have his hundredth birthday. If her hope was not utterly shattered, it must have hung by a very thin thread.

She was now an old woman, and no matter how often she and Abraham tried to conceive, the promise was still unfulfilled. Most women would have given up long before this. A lesser woman might have despaired of ever seeing the Lord's promise fulfilled. But Sarah "judged Him faithful who had promised" (Heb. 11:11 NKJV). This is why she is included in God's Hall of Faith.

God specifically brought Sarah for the first time into God's covenant with her husband in Genesis 17:15-16: God said to Abraham, "As for Sarai your wife, you are no longer to call her Sarai; her name will be Sarah. I will bless her and will surely give you a son by her. I will bless her so that she will be the mother of nations; kings of people will come from her." As God tested Sarah, he will test you. Learn to sincerely thank God for the future blessings even though you may need to wait for your new life in heaven with Jesus.

Sarah—A Good Host

The Lord visited Abraham in the form of three men. Abraham was anxious to serve them food and water which they accepted. "Abraham went into the tent to Sarah, 'Quick,' he said, 'get flour and knead it and bake some bread'" (Gen. 18:6). The men asked for Sarah and said to the couple, "I will surely return to you about this time next year, and Sarah will have a son." Sarah responded, "After I am worn out and my master is old, will I now have this pleasure?" (v. 12). For Sarah to refer to her husband as "master" was simply an expression of appreciation and recognition of her husband Abraham. She is not putting herself below Abraham; she is implying love for her husband.

Peter reflects on this incident, "Sarah obeyed Abraham and called him her master. You are her daughters if you do what is right" (I Peter 3:6). The women of Peter's time were wearing jewelry and fine clothes to catch the attention of men. Peter is saying that a woman's beauty of a gentle and quiet spirit does not fade but is of greater worth (than jewelry and fine clothes) in God's sight. (vv. 3-5).

Paul expresses this same principle in Ephesians 5:21, "Submit to one another out of reverence for Christ." He continues, "wives should submit to their husbands and husbands should love their wives as Christ loved the church and gave himself up for it." When husbands love their wives as their own bodies they treat their wives from a heart of love. As I say earlier, many men think they love their wives when they try to please them with things: money, vacations, jewelry and sharing the work load around the house, but when efforts are not from a heart of love, the wife does not feel loved. She wants more than your time, your money and service. She wants your heart. She wants to know you are her best friend. The same is true with God. We can serve God 24/7 and still not love God. Jesus said, "The greatest commandment is to love God with all your heart..." (Matt. 22:37-38).

Helen and I have been married 58 years. While we have had many days of struggles, our marriage is more fulfilling than it's ever been. We are best friends. We try to please each other. If you don't know Jesus, your love can only go so far. When we are in Jesus his eternal selfless love will overflow to your spouse. It's a wonderful relationship!

Repeated Mistakes

The same year that God destroyed Sodom and Gomorrah (Gen. 18:16–19:29), Abraham journeyed south again, this time into the land ruled by Abimelech, king of Gerar. Sarah, though now ninety, was still beautiful. She aroused the king's passion. What had happened in Egypt twenty-five years earlier was replayed once more. Abraham again tried to pass Sarah off as his sister, and Abimelech, smitten with her beauty, began to pursue her. But God spared Sarah, by warning Abimelech in a dream that she was Abraham's wife (Gen. 20:3). Abimelech was not permitted by God to touch her (v. 6), lest there be any question about whose child she would soon bear.

Abimelech, having been frightened when the Lord appeared to him in the dream, was gracious to Abraham and Sarah. He gave them silver and their choice of land. (vv.15-16).

"The Lord was gracious to Sarah... She became pregnant and bore a son to Abraham in his old age, at the very time God had promised him. Abraham gave the name Isaac to the son Sarah bore him... Sarah said, 'God has brought me laughter, and everyone who hears about this will laugh with me; [Isaac means he laughs]'" (Gen. 21:1-3 and 6). She saw genuine humor in the way God had dealt with her. She said, "Who would have said to Abraham that Sarah would nurse children? Yet I have borne him a son in his old age" (v. 7).

Despite Sarah's occasional bursts of temper with her handmaiden and Ishmael and her struggles with discouragement, Sarah remained an essentially good-humored woman. After those long years of bitter frustration, she could still appreciate the irony and relish the comedy of becoming a mother at such an old age. Her life's ambition was now realized, and the memory of years of bitter disappointment quickly disappeared from view. She forgot what was behind and pressed on to better things ahead. God had indeed been faithful.

Far too many Christians are hanging on to the years of disappointment and pain. Until they come to the cross and beg God to forgive them, the pain will remain. God will use every painful experience you have ever had to strengthen your faith if you surrender to him. God brought healing and joy to Sarah. Let him do the same for you.

ISAAC

A Willing Sacrifice

"By faith Isaac blessed Jacob and Esau in regard to their future" (Heb. 11:20). God kept his promise with the birth of Isaac when Abraham was 100 years old. Sarah was so ecstatic that she named him Isaac which means "he laughs." (Gen. 21:5-7). When Isaac was about to be weaned, Abraham had a great celebration. At the party, Ishmael and his mother, Hagar, made fun of Isaac. "Sarah turned to Abraham and demanded, 'Get rid of that slave-woman and her son. He is not going to share the inheritance with my son, Isaac. I won't have it!'" (vv. 8-10 NLT). Abraham grudgingly sent Hagar and Ishmael away but was comforted with God's promise to make Ishmael a great nation.

A Willing Sacrifice

When Isaac was in his teens, God told Abraham to go to Mt. Moriah and sacrifice his beloved son. Isaac, being a strong young man, allowed himself to be bound on the altar. We, like Isaac, must be willing to die ourselves and become a living sacrifice. (Ro. 12:1-2). We commit ourselves to be faithful to God in the morning, however some days before evening we crawl off the altar choosing to go our own self-centered way. We forget whose we are. We don't want to turn our backs on God's will but often we do.

In the first verse following the faith chapter of Hebrews 11, Paul gives us the secret for staying on the altar. "Since we are surrounded by such a great cloud of witnesses, let us throw off everything that hinders and the sin that so easily entangles, and let us run with perseverance the race marked out for us. Let us fix our eyes on Jesus, the author and perfecter of our faith, who for the joy set before him endured the cross, scorning its shame, and sat down at the right hand of the throne of God. Consider him who endured such opposition from sinful men so that you will not grow weary and lose heart. In your struggle against sin, you have not yet resisted to the point of shedding your blood. And you have forgotten the word of encouragement that addresses you as sons: 'My son, do not make light of the Lord's discipline, and do not lose heart when he rebukes you, because the Lord disciplines those he loves, and he punishes everyone he accepts as a son.'" (Heb. 12:1-6).

We are not alone; we are surrounded by a huge multitude of witnesses. If you have been to a college or professional football game, think of yourself in the arena with 100,000 people shouting for you to persevere to the finish. Paul describes perseverance: "Run to win. Athletics work hard to win a crown that cannot last, but we do it for a crown that will last forever. I don't run without a goal... l keep my body under control and make it my slave, so I won't lose out..." (I Cor. 9:24-27 CEV). Does that describe your life?

The New Testament reminds us we have been (notice the past tense) crucified with Christ. (Gal. 2:20). Seven times in Romans 6:1-11 Paul says we died when Christ died. We submit ourselves to the altar like Isaac. Augustine said, "Sin is believing the lie that we are self- created, self-dependent and self-sustained. Freedom is believing the truth that we are God-created, God-dependent and God sustained." This tests our faith. We want to believe but we struggle to apply this concept in our daily experience. Since we died, sin cannot have dominion over us. (Ro. 8). However, our human sinful nature is still alive. But because of Jesus' death and resurrection, the power to overcome our sin is present through our faith in him.

Dying to self is never easy. Jesus stayed on the "altar" dying for our sins. He conquered death by rising from the dead. Now we are privileged to place ourselves on the alter so others can see Christ in us. It's a choice we make daily. It's only in dying that we can live! Jesus said, "I tell you the truth, unless a kernel of wheat falls to the ground and dies, it remains only a single seed. But if it dies, it produces many seeds" (John 12:24).

I urge you, [I beg], you, (notice the plea Paul makes for us to get on the altar), in view of God's mercy to offer our bodies as living sacrifices, holy and pleasing to God. This is only reasonable considering what Jesus did for us. Don't conform to the patterns of this world, but be transformed by thinking God's thoughts. Then you can test and approve what is God's good and perfect will. (Romans 12:1-2).

When you are overlooked and don't receive the recognition you feel you deserve can you stay on the altar? When your friend betrays you or you get a note that your job is terminated, can you stay on the altar? Every day we choose if we are going to stay on the altar or go our own self-centered way. Jesus said, "If anyone would come after me, he must deny himself and take up his cross daily (stay on the altar) and follow me" (Luke 9:23).

Sometimes when the trials seem insurmountable we may want God to just take us home. If he would honor that desire our witness here would be of little value. How much greater is your witness if you keep yourselves on the altar as a living sacrifice! We are living witnesses of what God can do through our trials and hardships as we trust his power to deliver us in his time. Noah stayed on the altar for 120 years. You can too.

The Second Most Important Decision

Who you choose for a marriage partner is the second most important decision of your life. The first is your decision to invite Christ to control your life. God designed for some to remain celibate for life. They are definitely not second-class citizens as they are often treated. As Paul, who was living a celibate life writes, they are free to serve God while those who choose marriage must also please their spouse. (I Cor. 7:32-34).

Before Abraham died he wanted to be sure his son, Isaac, did not marry a local Canaanite woman but a woman from God's chosen people, a follower of Jehovah. (Gen. 24). Abraham sent his servant, a distance of several hundred miles, to find a wife for Isaac. The servant was concerned that he may not be able to find a willing young woman to return with him. Abraham promised his servant an angel would go with him to find a wife. Abraham's servant took additional servants and ten camels loaded with the finest of gifts for the woman who was willing to return with him.

When they arrived at Aram-naharaim, he found the village where Abraham's brother, Nahor had settled. Abraham's servant found a well and made his camels kneel down to wait for water. Women were coming to draw water. Abraham's servant prayed that when he asked one of the women for a drink she would not only give water to his men but to the camels as well.

Rebecca arrived, a water jug on her shoulder. She filled the jug. Abraham's servant asked her for a drink. She quickly lowered the jug for him to drink. When he finished, she offered to water the camels. He gave her a gold ring and bracelets. As the servant dialogued with her he learned she was Abraham's great niece. Rebecca ran to tell her brother, Laban what occurred. Laban immediately invited Abraham's servant and his team to stay overnight. Abraham's servant related why they came. Laban instantly recognized God's providence.

Abraham was confident God would see to it that his servants' mission would be successful. As we grow in faith we learn to hear God's voice. (John 10:4, 27). For those who walk with God there is no such thing as coincidence. God directs our steps (Ps. 37:23). "Trust in the Lord with all your heart, do not depend on your own understanding. Seek his will in all you do, and he will direct your paths." (Prov. 3:5-6 NLT). We, like Abraham and his servant, can walk in faith and confidence today. The supernatural will become natural. I experience his leading every day. Stay on the altar and you will experience peace and joy beyond description.

In the morning, Abraham's servant requested that Rebecca come with him. Rebecca consented. As the servant returned with Rebecca, God arranged for Isaac to see them approaching.

Isaac was forty when he married Rebecca. Isaac pleaded with the Lord to grant them children. Rebecca became pregnant with twins, Jacob and Esau. As they grew Esau loved the out-of-doors and the freedom of the open fields. Not surprisingly he became a skillful hunter, (Gen. 25:27). His twin brother Jacob was the opposite. He was content to stay home among the tents. Spending his time with Rebecca cooking savory meals.

Partiality Brings Suffering

Isaac, who had a taste for wild game, loved Esau, but Rebecca loved Jacob. As we have seen before, favoritism on the part of the parents always leads to jealousy, resentment and causes serious friction. The consequences are often carried from one generation to the next. Moses reminds us that the sins of the fathers are passed on to the third and fourth generation. (Deut. 5:9). Paul's instruction to Timothy is still needed today. "Do not show partiality" (I Tim. 5:21).

Certain holidays, especially Thanksgiving, Christmas, Easter, and Fourth of July, when families get together, depression and suicide often increases. Many have deep-rooted hurts from childhood caused by parents showing partiality. Parents and children live with guilt affecting their quality of life.

Circumstance Force Change

A famine occurred, (Ch. 26) so Isaac moved his family to the Philistine territory under King Abimelech. Isaac was afraid King Abimelech would take his wife Rebekah into his harem. He learned from his father, Abraham, how to handle this situation. Our sins are so often passed to our children. Isaac told everyone that Rebekah was his sister so they would not kill him and take Rebekah. One day King Abimelech saw Isaac caressing Rebekah. (26:8). The King was conscience stricken and gave orders that anyone making trouble for Rebekah would be put to death.

The famine forced Isaac to move. Today floods, fires, hurricanes, tsunamis and famines and other natural disaster force people to move. How should we react when these occur? First do not say this occurred because of their sin. (Luke 13:1-3). Pray for those in harm's way to experience strength from God to rise above their devastation. Pray for God to send workers and for people to be willing to go and help. Pray that the gifts will bring hope and open hearts to receive God love in the midst of their loss. Pray for God's people to give generously. And pray that people would be given wisdom concerning ways they might either prevent further disasters or be better prepared to sustain future disasters.

Overcoming Evil with Good

The Philistines were jealous of Isaac because he became wealthy. They took revenge by stopping up the wells that Abraham's servants had dug. Plugging up a well was a clear sign of war. It was saying, "you are not wanted here. This is our land."

King Abimelech ordered Isaac to leave his country. Isaac moved to the valley of Gerar. (26:17). He cleared out wells that the Philistines had stopped up. His servants dug another well, but the local shepherds claimed the water. Isaac's servants dug another well with the same results. Finally, they dug yet another well and named it "Rehoboth" meaning the Lord has made room for us. We will be fruitful.

Isaac conquered evil by doing good. (Rom. 12:21). This universal principle runs throughout Scripture. "A gentle answer turns away wrath, but a harsh word stirs up anger" (Prov. 15:1). Gentle speech breaks down rigid defenses" (Prov. 15:15 Msg). Elijah overcame evil with good. When he was surrounded by the Syrian Army, he prayed. The Lord blinded the enemy and Elijah prepared a banquet for the Syrian army and sent them home. The war ceased. (II Kings. 6:8-23).

Jesus said that we are to love our enemies and pray for them. If we do this we will be imitating our Father in heaven. (Matt. 5:44). He taught us to go the second mile, i.e. to put our enemies to shame by doing more for them than they expected. (Matt. 5:40-41). This second-mile service will often get people's attention. "Why are they treating us kindly? Why are we harming them?" When Jesus was on the cross he prayed for his enemies. Paul reminds us to do good to everyone and to overcome evil by doing good. (Gal. 6:10; Rom. 12:21). Even if you don't feel like doing good, do it anyway because you know what Jesus wants you to do and eventually the feelings will follow.

How many wars would be obliterated if we would overcome evil with good? Family wars, church wars, wars in our places of employment, in our communities and even world wars! Jesus said, "Blessed are the peacemakers." (Matt. 5:9).

JACOB
A Life of Conflict

HEBREWS 11:21

Esau came home exhausted and starved from a hunt. He said to his younger brother Jacob, "I'm starved! Give me some of that red stew!" (Gen. 25:29-30). Jacob agreed on the condition that Esau give up his birthright. The birthright entitled the oldest son in the family to receive a double portion of the family's inheritance and become the head of the family taking his father's position. Esau didn't hesitate. He says: "Who cares about a birthright when you are famished?"

Paul warns: "Watch out that no poisonous root of bitterness grows up to trouble you, corrupting many. Make sure that no one is immoral or godless like Esau, who traded his birthright as the first-born son for a single meal. You know that afterwards when he wanted his father's blessing, he was rejected, it was too late for repentance, even though he begged with bitter tears" (Heb. 12:15-17 NLT). "Watch out for the Esau syndrome: trading away God's lifelong gift in order to satisfy a short-term appetite" (Heb. 12:16 Msg.).

Before Isaac died he called for his first-born son Esau to take his bow and bring some game home. He instructed Esau to make a delicious meal then he would give his son his blessings. Rebecca overheard Isaac giving Esau instructions, so he could bless him. Rebecca planned to have her favorite son, Jacob, receive Isaac's blessing rather than Esau. Jacob foolishly agrees to her plan to steal his brother's birthright. Rebecca helped Jacob prepare a delicious meal and take it to his father pretending to be Esau. To pull off this disguise Rebecca had Jacob cover himself with hairy lamb skin, so his skin would feel like Esau's. When Jacob approached his father, Isaac believed he was hearing Jacob's voice not Esau's, but the hairy skin and the lies from Jacob's lips convinced his nearly blind father Isaac to bless him. This meant that Jacob would become the spiritual leader of the family following Isaac's death as well as inheriting the promises of Abraham. (Gen. 27 and 28).

A bit later when Esau returned from his hunt, he prepared Isaac's favorite meal and brought it to him awaiting his father's blessing. On hearing his father had given his blessing to Jacob, Esau was frantic and vowed to kill his brother Jacob (Gen. 27:4). Jacob's mother Rebecca comes to the rescue again by insisting Jacob immediately move a great distance away to work for his uncle Laban. (28:5). Jacob fled leaving his Father's wealth to Esau. Jacob then works as Laban's servant. Although Jacob deceived Isaac by stealing Esau's birthright and blessing, now Jacob experiences deception from his Uncle Laban. "Be sure your sin will find you out." (Numbers 32:23).

Delayed Gratification

Human nature says, "I like what I see. I want it now." We want immediate gratification rather than eternal blessings. Television ads encourage us to get what we want and get it today, no money down for 18 months. Delayed gratification is a discipline that seems forgotten in our world, especially in the younger generation. Only fifty percent of young adults have a saving account to carry them over for more than a week. They live from paycheck to paycheck not being willing to deny themselves whatever they want. Today many have become slaves to their charge cards ignoring the fact of double-digit interest. There is little self-restraint or self-control as they are seemingly blind to their bondage.

Jesus constantly emphasizes self-denial. "The key to self-fulfillment is self-denial. Self-denial is shorthand for delayed gratification. By delay, I don't mean days or months or years. I mean a lifetime. Our delayed gratification on earth translates into eternal glory in heaven. The selfish part of us has an allergic reaction to the word deny. It's tough to do when we live in the lap of luxury. We don't just tolerate indulgence in our culture; we celebrate it. But the fundamental problem with indulgence is that enough is never enough. The more we indulge ourselves in food or sex or the amenities of wealth, the less we will enjoy them. It's not until we go all in with God that we discover that true joy is only found on the sacrificial side of life" (Mark Batterson, *All In*. Zondervan, 2013. p.26).

Romance

Jacob fell in love with Laban's daughter Rachel. Laban agrees to give Rachel to Jacob in marriage on the condition he work seven years for Rachel. He worked those seven years but following the marriage ceremony the veiled woman in his bed was Leah, Rachel's older sister. Uncle Laban insists he work another seven years for Rachel which he did because he greatly loved Rachel.

Jacob's flocks multiplied which made Laban envious. As tension mounted, God came to Jacob and told him to return to his father's and grandfathers' homeland. (Gen. 31:3). Jacob now becomes exceedingly fearful as he thinks of meeting Esau whom he has cheated remembering Esau's vow to kill him. He wrestles with God all night in prayer. Still being fearful, Jacob decides to appease Esau by sending waves of gifts to Esau as they come near to each other. Jacob bows before Esau showing remorse. He insists Esau receive his gifts. God's plan is worked out in spite of Jacob's many sins.

Wrestling in Prayer

Jacob, wrestling with God in prayer, is one of the most challenging verses concerning prayer in the bible. (Genesis 32:24-30). Wrestling with God in prayer results in repentance. Without repentance you cannot receive God's forgiveness and grace. Reconciliation will cost us our self-centered ego, but the peace that follows is far greater than living with inner turmoil. God was not defeated. (Gen. 25:23). Jacob was to be the one carrying the family name and God brought that about in spite of Jacob's many detours. God can redeem our rebellion and stubbornness. No sin is so great for God to redeem if we are willing to come in humility, brokenness and repentance. God renamed Jacob calling him "Israel" which means one who wrestles with God. (Gen. 35:10).

When you are at odds with anyone, do what Jacob did: wrestle with God in prayer. Then do what God tells you to do. Even if your adversary does not accept your efforts to bring reconciliation, if you do what God wants you to do, you receive his peace and blessing. Jesus said, "Blessed are the peacemakers for they will be called sons of God" (Matt. 5:9). Just hours before his crucifixion Jesus told his disciples, "Peace I leave with you; my peace I give you. I do not give to you as the world gives. Do not let your hearts be troubled and do not be afraid" (John 14:27). Notice it is not your peace, it is Jesus giving you his peace. Our human fleshly peace is temporal and shallow.

From Paul's prison cell he writes. "Don't worry about anything, but pray about everything. With thankful hearts offer up your prayers and requests to God. Then because you belong to Christ Jesus, God will bless you with peace that no one can completely understand. And this peace will control the way you think and feel" (Phil. 4:6-7 CEV). Peace is a fruit of the Holy Spirit. (Gal. 5:22). God will give you peace if you fix your mind on him. (Isaiah 26:3).

Jesus, in the Garden of Gethsemane, agonized in prayer. (Luke 22:44). Paul used the same root word to describe his pain as he wrestles with God in his passion to present everyone mature in Christ Jesus. "I want you to know how much I have agonized for you...and for many other friends who have never known me" (Col. 2:1 NLT). Oh, that we would be willing to wrestle with God.

"Prayer is not primarily God's way of getting things done. It is God's way of giving the Church 'on-the-job' training in overcoming the forces hostile to God. The world is a laboratory in which those destined for the throne are learning, by actual practice in the prayer closet, how to overcome Satan and his hierarchy. God designed the program of prayer as an 'apprenticeship' for eternal sovereignty with Christ."[17] (Billheimer, *Destined for the Throne*. p. 40).

Veteran Missionary, Don Jacobs writes, "We Christians discover that our most powerful weapon against Satan is fervent prayer. When I asked some Ethiopians why their church grew so much during their 10 years of severe persecution (1982-1992), they all responded; 'We learned to pray out of our desperation.' We might think that persecution produces growth. That might be, but the heart of the matter is that persecution drives saints to give themselves to imploring prayer, because they can simply do nothing about the situation. Churches around the world are rediscovering the mighty power of prayer. Entire congregations are praying aloud; all at once for a long time, praying fervently, begging in fact.

17 Paul Billheimer, *Destined for the Throne*. Christian Literature Crusade, Fort Washington, PA, 1975. p. 40.

They are experiencing the truth of Jesus' invitation to ask… seek… and knock" (Matt. 7:7)."[18]

Prayer and passion are couplets. A lack of prayer reveals lack of passion and a lack of passion reveals a lack of prayer. David, the man after God's own heart, reveals his passion: "As the deer pants for the streams of water, so my soul pants for you, O God" (Ps. 42:1). "I open my mouth and pant, longing for your commands" (119:141). "You will seek me and find me when you seek me with all your heart" (Jeremiah 29:13). Hannah prayed out of great languishing and sorrow and the Lord granted her request. (I Sam. 15:30). Samuel begged and pleaded with the Lord, and the Lord defeated the Philistines. (I Sam. 7:9). Elijah was a great man of God and he stood alone against 850 false prophets but James reminds us that Elijah was a man just like us. God rewards those who earnestly (passionately) seek him. (Heb. 11:6). The prayer of a righteous man is powerful and effective" (James 5:17).

The late Bill Bright said, "It is my strong conviction that it is impossible to ask God for too much if our hearts and motives are pure, and if we pray according to the Word and will of God… Whatever we vividly envision, ardently desire, sincerely believe and enthusiastically act upon will come to pass, assuming of course, that there is spiritual authority for it. It is this principle that is the foundation of praying supernaturally."

---

18 Don Jacobs, "Into All the World" pp. 184-185.

JOSEPH

From Pit to Prime Minister

HEBREWS 11:22

Joseph was number eleven of the twelve boys born to Jacob. He had one sister. Jacob loved Joseph more than the other children, since he was born in his old age. (Gen. 37:3). His brothers resented Joseph because of the preferential treatment he received from his father. Making matters worse was Joseph's dreams he unwisely shared with his family. We were binding sheaves of grain. Each of my eleven brother's sheaves bowed down to my sheaf. In another dream he said, "Listen, this time the sun and moon and eleven stars were bowing down to me." (Gen. 37:9). Their hatred increased because of this dream. His father, Jacob, rebuked Joseph but that did not change his siblings' attitude toward Joseph.

Joseph's brothers were tending their flocks forty miles away near Shechem. Jacob sent Joseph to see how they were getting along. When they saw Joseph coming, they plotted to kill him. But Reuben, the oldest brother, tried to spare his life by suggesting they throw him into a cistern.

Reuben's plan to rescue him failed. God directed a caravan of Ishmaelite merchants to pass by continuing on their 30-40 day journey to Egypt. Judah suggested they sell Joseph to these traders for twenty pieces of silver. They stripped off Joseph's special coat his father had given him and sent him with the caravan of Ishmaelites. Dipping Joseph's coat in animal blood they returned it to their father. Jacob was convinced a wild animal had killed his beloved son. (Gen. 37:35).

Favoritism Rears Its Ugly Head Again

Like father, like son. Jacob commits the sin of showing partiality just like his father Isaac had done to him and his brother Esau.

Partiality continues to bring devastation to multitudes of families today. Parents need to make every effort to treat each child in the way they feel their parent's love. Every child is different. As Christian parents we must ask God for wisdom to know how to express our love so each child feels loved and secure. "Train up a child in the way they should go and in keeping with their individual gifts or bent, and when they are old they will not depart from it" (Prov. 22:6 AMP).

Jesus chose twelve disciples. Peter, James and John were in the inside circle of Jesus' close friendship. John was the beloved disciple. Were the other disciples jealous of this inner circle? Jesus was able to identify with all the disciples so they felt loved just as much as Peter, James and John.

The ten disciples became angry when James and John wanted to have reserved seats beside Jesus in heaven. The ten became angry. "Jesus called them together and said: 'You know that those foreigners who call themselves kings like to order the people around. And their great leaders have full power over the people they rule. But don't act like them. If you want to be great, you must be the servant of all the others. And if you want to be first, you must be everyone's slave. The Son of Man did not come to be a slave master, but a slave, who will give his life to rescue many people'" (Mark 10:41-45 CEV). Jesus is clear, both parties need to correct their thinking. He lifted all of them to a higher level of living to overcome their jealousy.

Joseph, in his immaturity, fueled the jealousy of his siblings by delightfully, and I suspect boastfully, sharing his dreams. Learn to guard your tongue so you don't put salt in wounds that are already present. We love to be in the spotlight, but pride goes before destruction. (Prov. 16:18). We are to be quick to listen and slow to speak. (James 1:19).

God Directs the Midianites

The Midianites sold Joseph to Potiphar, the kings' officer. (Gen. 39). The Lord blessed Joseph with wisdom so that everything in Potiphar's household greatly prospered. Admiring Joseph's physique, Potiphar's wife became infatuated with Joseph. She consistently begged him to have sex with her. Joseph stayed away from her as much as possible. She set a trap catching him when he was alone in the house and pressured him. He refused, "How could I do such a wicked thing and sin against God?" (Gen. 39:9).

Joseph understood what most people even in the New Testament do not understand. Sin is against God. He understood the seriousness of sin and what it meant to fear the Lord. Today we have deliberately lost the word "sin" from our vocabulary. There are seventeen catalogues or lists of sins in the New Testament listing more than fifty specific sins. The Greek word, "hamartano" means to miss the mark. In our New Testament the word "sin" appears 220 times occurring in nearly every book of the New Testament. Nearly thirty sins are listed in Romans 1 while Galatians 5 lists twenty. The most prevalent sin among the catalogues of sin is sexual immorality which often heads the list and is demonstrated by Potiphar's wife and by Hollywood today.

Pornography is running wild in America. According to Wikipedia.org the porn industry income is $10-12 billion in the U.S. Child porn is a $3 billion industry." Jesus lists many specific sins. In Matt. 15:18-29 he specifies "evil thoughts, murder, adultery, sexual immorality, theft, false testimony, slander." Until we are willing to call acts of sin, "sin" our churches will be insipid and powerless to challenge our culture.

The Fear or Reverence of God Is Meant to Keep Us from Sin

We have lost the fear of God. "Job feared God and shunned evil" (Job 1:1, 8). "Fear the Lord and shun evil" (Prov. 3:7). "To fear the Lord is to hate evil" (Prov. 8:13). "Through the fear of the Lord evil is avoided" (Prov. 16:6). "When the people saw the thunder and lightning and heard the trumpet and saw the mountain in smoke they trembled with fear... Moses said to the people. 'Do not be afraid. God has come to test you, so that the fear of God will be with you to keep you from sinning'" (Exodus 20:18-20). They were to keep the fear of God in their minds so they would not sin.

Today when most people think of God they think of him as being detached. Some see God as a God of love who overlooks sin. Paul writes to the Ephesians: "All of us lived among them at one time, gratifying the cravings of our sinful nature and following its desires and thoughts. Like the rest we were by nature objects of wrath" (Eph. 2:3).

Most Americans never think of themselves as being objects of God's wrath. Christians think of God as a God of love ignoring the justice of God. Therefore, we don't fear, respect or have reverence for God. There is a clear link between a lack of fear of God and the loose, immoral living engaged in today. "Let us purify ourselves from everything that contaminates body and spirit, perfecting holiness out of reverence for God" (II Cor. 7:1). The NLT reads: "Let us work toward complete purity because we fear God."

"Satan knows our desires and offers to meet them in ways that seem innocuous and harmless. If we could see the results of sin before choosing it, we wouldn't choose it. We know that 'the wages of sin is death' (Romans 6:23), but it seems hard at the time to believe that this warning applies to us. There's a voice that encourages us to believe that no one will be hurt by what we're considering." (Jim Denison blog, March 14, 2018). A reverent respect for God will help us say "no" to the desires of our evil nature and the onslaughts of the Satanic evil forces.

Testing Time

Potiphar's wife lied to her husband informing him that Joseph pursued her. Potiphar chose to believe his wife. In his fury he imprisoned Joseph. Jesus said we are blessed when people revile us and say all manner of false statements against us. Then he adds that we are to rejoice and be supremely joyful because we have a great reward in heaven awaiting us. (Matt. 5:10-12). Jesus is saying that we may have to wait to receive this great reward when we get to heaven. Like Jesus, Joseph did not defend himself. He trusted God to defend him. (I Pet. 2:23).

We need to prepare ourselves for false accusations so that when they come, we will not be caught unaware. Jesus reminded us that we are not to be surprised if the world hates us. (I John 3:13). The world hates us because we do not belong to the world. (John 15:19 and 17:14). "If you are insulted because of the name of Christ, you are blessed… Those who suffer according to God's will should commit themselves to their faithful Creator and continue to do good." (I Peter 4:14, 19).

God's Presence

God never forsakes his people. "While Joseph was imprisoned the Lord was with him; he showed him kindness and granted him favor in the eyes of the prison warden... and God gave him success in whatever he did." (Gen. 39:21-23). Jesus promised to be with us. His presence brings peace and joy in the midst of painful persecutions. He assured us that if we remain in the vine, i.e. in him, his joy in us will be complete. (John 15:11, 17:13)). His joy becomes our joy. His peace becomes our peace. "Peace I leave with you, my peace I give you... Do not let your heart be troubled and do not be afraid." (John 14:27). "You will keep in perfect peace those whose minds are steadfast (stayed on you) because they trust in you." (Isaiah 16:3).

God Uses Unbelievers to Open the Door to Freedom

Pharaoh's cupbearer and baker were in prison with Joseph because they had offended Pharaoh. They each had a dream which Joseph correctly interpreted. (Gen. 40). Two years later Pharaoh had two dreams, but all the magicians and wise men could not interpret them. (Gen. 41). Then the cupbearer remembered Joseph. Pharaoh told Joseph the dreams and God gave him the interpretation. Pharaoh was so impressed he placed Joseph in charge of his palace and all the people. (v. 40).

Perseverance

God's timing is often different than our timing. Joseph was Pharaoh's slave at age 17. He had to wait 13 years to become Pharaoh's right-hand man. Perseverance is one of the primary characteristics of a disciple of Jesus. Paul commends the Thessalonians "Among God's churches we boast about your perseverance and faith in all the persecutions and trials you are enduring" (II Thess. 1:4). The testing of our faith develops perseverance resulting in maturity. (James 1:3-4). Jesus commends the churches of Ephesus and Thyatira for their perseverance. (Rev. 2:2 and 19). "We rejoice in our sufferings because suffering produces perseverance; perseverance character...." (Rom. 5:3-4). Peter writes that we are to add perseverance to our faith so we will be productive and effective. (II Pet. 1:6-8). We are admonished to get rid of all sin so we can run with perseverance and patience the race before us, keeping our eyes on Jesus who endured appalling suffering. (Heb.12:1-3).

Suffering is overcome as God enables us to persevere. Paul who suffered horrific pain and torture says, "I consider that our present sufferings are not worth comparing with the glory that will be revealed in us. (Romans 8:18).

Restoration at Last

As Joseph predicted there was a seven-year famine. Jacob learned there was grain in Egypt. Joseph's brothers all went to Egypt except Benjamin, Joseph's younger brother. When they arrived, Joseph recognized his brothers, but they did not recognize him. He accused them of being spies and imprisoned them for three days. He sent them home with grain but kept Simon. Joseph insisted that they were not to return unless they brought their younger brother Benjamin.

It wasn't long before Jacob's family was on the verge of starvation. Jacob insisted they go to Egypt for food. After assuring Jacob that they cannot return unless Benjamin accompanies them, Jacob finally consented. This time Joseph revealed himself to his brothers. They were afraid that Joseph would take revenge. He said to them, "Don't be afraid. Am I in the place of God? You intended it to harm me, but God intended it for good to accomplish what is now being done, the saving of many lives. I will provide for you and your children. And he assured them and spoke kindly to them." (Gen. 50:19-21).

All of us have been treated unfairly at times: perhaps by an employer, your family, an unfaithful spouse, you may have been sexually molested or scarred with emotional and physical pain. Many, because of the color of their skin, have been treated unfairly. Your pain cannot be healed unless you forgive your perpetrators as Joseph forgave his brothers. Jesus said, "For if you forgive other people when they sin against you, your heavenly Father will also forgive you. But if you do not forgive others their sins, your heavenly Father will not forgive your sins." (Matt. 6:14-15). Pour your heart out to God asking him to help you forgive. No matter how often you said, "I will not forgive." God's love and grace enable you to forgive. It may take time to feel love for those who harmed you but as you grow in your walk with Jesus you will be amazed at the attitude of love that transcends your understanding. Thank God for his forgiving grace.

MOSES

Learning to Look Ahead—Overcoming Fear

HEB. 11:23-29

Pharaoh realized that the Israelites were multiplying and would soon dominate Egypt. He put the Israelites under slave masters to oppress them with ruthless labor, however the more he oppressed them the more they multiplied. (Exodus 1:12).

In desperation he ordered his midwives to kill all the Israelite baby boys. The midwives feared God and let the boys live. (1:17). God was kind to the midwives and the people became even more numerous. Pharaoh's next strategy was to drown all the baby boys in the Nile River. (1:22).

Abortion

Since 1973 nearly 50 million babies were aborted in our nation. God honored the midwives who said, "No" to Pharaoh." God honors the parents today who say "No" to aborting their babies. Science is clear that life begins at conception but in this unusual turn of events many in our culture deny our "god" science and take a self-centered route in narcissism. Paul writes: "The minds of godless people are in the dark, and they are stubborn and ignorant and have missed out on the life that comes from God. They no longer have any feelings about what is right" (Eph.4:18 CEV). The good news is, our gracious God extends mercy, forgiveness and healing to those who are truly sorry for the murder of these unborn children.

When Moses' mother, Jochebed, could no longer hide her child, she prepared a papyrus basket and placed him among the reeds of the Nile. His sister, Miriam, watched over him. Pharaoh's daughter arrived to bathe and discovered the baby. Her heart was touched. Miriam came out of hiding and asked Pharaoh's daughter if she would like a Hebrew woman to nurse the baby. Miriam arranged for Moses' mother to care for him until he was weaned. Pharaoh's daughter adopted the child and named him Moses which means he was drawn out of the water. (Exodus 2:1-10).

Obey God Rather than Human Authority

Moses' parents had courageously defied the king. We need to say "No" to anyone who asks us to disobey God's will. Does your employer ask you to tweak the records so the company reports look good? Do you falsify your income when you prepare your taxes? Do you hide the fact that you are a follower of Jesus knowing your peers don't respect God? Do you teach your children by word and example to be truthful even though others will make fun of them? Israel's leaders repeatedly told the people to pass on to the next generation the commands of the Lord to revere and obey his word. (Ps. 78:1-8; Deut. 6:1-9). Your greatest mission field is your family.

Running Ahead of God

As an adult Moses observed the cruel labor of his people. He saw an Egyptian beating a fellow Israelite. Taking things into his own hands he killed the Egyptian. The next day two Hebrew men were fighting. When he intervened one of the men said, "Are you going to kill me like you killed the Egyptian?" Moses realized Pharaoh might hear what happened. He fled to Midian where God allowed him to feed sheep in the desert for 40 years. God was preparing Moses to lead his people to freedom. Moses had to realize that his plans were not God's plans. After forty years of training in God's school he was ready for his next level in God's school.

Humility

God called Moses to deliver his people. Numbers 12:3 describes Moses as "a very humble man, more humble than anyone else on the face of earth." It appears Moses went to the other extreme when God asked him to speak to the King. He begged God to send someone else. (Exodus 4:10-14). When God asks us to do something we must learn to say as Paul, "I will do everything through him who gives me strength" (Phil. 4:13).

How do we discern between humility and self-centered pride? "Do not think of yourself more highly than you ought, but rather think of yourself with sober judgment, in accordance with the measure of faith God has given you" (Rom. 12:3). When someone complements you, do not devalue what you have done. Give glory to God for enabling you to do what he asks. Don't promote yourself or belittle yourself. God created you with unique gifts to use for his glory. Don't make light of these gifts or think that you are superior to others because of God's gifts to you. Use your gifts to honor God.

On the other hand, don't seek humility by thinking everyone else is better than you when the obvious evidence is to the contrary. Find your security in Christ, he loves you as much as he loves his Son. (John 17:23, 26). In his security you are free to love others, without feeling superior or inferior. You can offer grace by showing genuine care. You can love others as you love yourself.

Isaiah was not the only one who made excuses. God called Jeremiah to be his "prophet to the nations" (Jer. 1:5), he responded: "Alas, Sovereign Lord ... I do not know how to speak, I am too young." "But the Lord said, "Do not say, 'I am too young,' You must go to everyone I send you to and say whatever I commend you. Do not be afraid of them, for I'm with you and will rescue you,' declares the Lord" (Jer. 1:6-8).

God can do more through you than you can think or imagine. (Eph. 3:20-21). He designed you to soar like eagles, not grovel in the dust. Learn to say like Isaiah. "Here I am, send me" (Is. 6:8). When Corrie ten Boom was fearful to get on the train that she knew was taking her to the death camp, she remembers her father's word that God would provide grace when she needed it. Corrie ten Boom has said to the effect, why are we content to swim in a backyard mud puddle when God has an ocean of inexhaustible grace for us? When we resist doing God's will, we are admitting our lack of faith or perhaps even our laziness and cowardness. Many Christians grieve God's Holy Spirit because they are unwilling to do what they know they should do. (Eph. 4:30). Don't deny God's call by labeling your reaction as humility. This cuts the joy and power God wants to give you.

God Empowered Moses

God instructed Moses what to say to Pharaoh. He promised Moses that the Egyptians would free the Israelites and send them away with silver and gold and all they needed. God also promised to provide signs/miracles to verify his promises. (Ex. 3-4). These miracles of ten plagues finally convinced Pharaoh to send the Israelites away. (Each of the plagues were designed to demonstrate that Israel's God was superior to the Egyptian gods.)

What is God asking you to do? Is he asking you to help your neighbor or take time to speak to those who are lonely? As we are tuned into God's Spirit, he not only impresses on our mind what he wants us to do but he often accompanies his request with signs such as perfect timing so we realize that the encounter was not a mere coincidence. "In all your ways acknowledge him and he will direct your steps." (Prov. 3:6 KJV). When we obey God, the supernatural becomes natural.

Support from Others

Moses felt inadequate to approach Pharaoh, so God provided his brother Aaron to come beside him to assist him. When you feel inadequate, ask others for their prayers, council and assistance. (Eph. 5:21). Jesus sent his disciples out by two's. When we feel alone in battling the principalities and powers, we need the whole armor of God as well as the prayers and assistance of others. (Eph. 6:10-20).

God Is Sovereign

God hardened Pharaoh's heart. (Exodus 9:12). Since God knows all things, he knew Pharaoh would not submit to their request to leave Egypt, therefore he speaks of it as if it has already happened. "For those God foreknew he also predestined to be conformed to the likeness of his Son" (Rom. 8:29). Our finite minds will never fully understand God's omniscience (all knowingness) and his sovereignty.

The daily news reminds us of what is happening among the nations of our world. God is in control. "The king's heart is in the hand of the Lord; he directs it like a watercourse wherever he pleases" (Prov. 21:1). God humbled Nebuchadnezzar until Nebuchadnezzar "acknowledges that the Most High God is sovereign over the kingdoms of men and sets over them anyone he wishes" (Dan 5:21c; 4:25). Jehoshaphat said: "O Lord God... you rule over all the kingdoms of the nations. Power and might are in your hand, and no one can withstand you" (II Chron. 20:5-6).

"The nations are as a drop in a bucket and are counted as the small dust of the balance. All nations before Him are as nothing and they are counted by Him as less than nothing and meaningless. It is God who sits upon the circle of the earth, who stretches out the heavens as a curtain and spreads them out as a tent to dwell in, and the inhabitants are as grasshoppers. He brings the princes to nothing. He makes the judges of the earth meaningless... he will blow on them, and they will wither, and the whirlwind will take them away as stubble." (Excerpts from Isaiah 40:15-24).

"Let all the earth fear the Lord; let all the people of the world revere him. For he spoke, and it came to be; he commanded, and it stood firm. The Lord foils the plans of the nations; he thwarts the purpose of the people. But the plans of the Lord stand firm forever, the purposes of his heart through all generations. Blessed is the nation whose God is the Lord... From heaven the Lord looks down and sees all mankind; he watches all who live on earth—he who forms the hearts of all, who considers everything they do. No king is saved by the size of his army; no warrior escapes his great strength. A horse is a vain hope for deliverance; despite all his great strength it cannot save, but the eyes of the Lord are on those who fear him on those whose hope is in his unfailing love, to deliver them from death" (Psalm 33:8-19a).

No matter how large our armies or powerful our weapons, God will determine the result. We don't worship our nation or put our faith in the military but in the King of Kings. Our help is in the Lord. (Heb. 13:5-6). "Some trust in chariots and some in horses, but we trust in the name of the Lord our God." (Ps. 20:7). "I am the Lord All-Powerful. Don't depend on your own power or strength, but on my Spirit" (Zechariah 4:6 CEV). God engraves us on the palm of his hand. (Is. 49:16). We are safe there! Stay there!

Primary Allegiance

As a disciple of Jesus, your first allegiance is to God's Kingdom, for he is King of Kings. "God has rescued us from the dominion of darkness and brought us into the kingdom of the Son he loves" (Col. 1:13). "My kingdom is not of this world, if it were, my servants would fight to prevent my arrest by the Jews. But now my kingdom is from another place" (John 18:36). Give your allegiance to God's eternal Kingdom even though it may cost you your earthly life.

Perseverance

Moses persevered by repeatedly going to challenge Pharaoh and then to his own people promising them God would deliver them. Their deliverance was not immediate. We want immediate deliverance but God will give us patience. God's timing is his tool to develop our faith. Joseph had to wait 13 years before God delivered him from prison. You may need to stay in your present situation indefinitely or even until you die. Tell God you will be faithful no matter what he asks. As Job said, "Though he slay me yet will I trust him" (Job. 13:15 KJV).

Blood Is Indispensable

"By faith Moses left Egypt, not fearing the king's anger; he persevered because he saw him who is invisible. By faith he kept the Passover and the sprinkling of blood, so that the destroyer of the firstborn would not touch the firstborn of Israel." (Heb. 11:27-28). The last plague God sent upon the Egyptians was the death of the first-born in every family. Every Israelite household needed to slaughter a lamb and place the blood on the doorposts and mantel of their house so the death angel would pass-over their house. (Exodus 12). God did not say, "place the blood on the door" he said to place the blood on the door posts and on the lintel. Placing blood in these three spots is perhaps a prophetic picture of the cross of Christ.

Blood is central to God's plan of redemption. In our "intellectual" culture, it's often repulsive to speak about the blood of Jesus needed to cover our sin. "Without the shedding of blood there is no forgiveness." (Heb. 9:22). "The life of a creature is in the blood, and I have given it to you to make atonement for yourselves on the altar; it is the blood that makes atonement for one's life" (Lev. 17:11). The cross is the most widely known symbol in our world however even those who wear a cross often don't know Jesus. We must trust Jesus atoning death and resurrection to have his eternal life in us.

How does the blood of Jesus apply to us today? Anesthesia was discovered in past generations, but it works for us today. Jesus blood covered our sins for all time. We celebrate Holy Communion or the Eucharist which is a service of thanksgiving for Jesus who gave his life's blood as the Lamb of God sacrificed to cover our sin. Just as the lambs of the Israelites had to be perfect, so Jesus is our perfect lamb.

Paul says, "I resolved to know nothing while I was with you except Jesus Christ and him crucified" (I Cor. 2:2). There is no salvation apart from the cross. The blood is a red cord that runs from Genesis to Revelation. It's the theme that unlocks the Bible. "He was pierced for our transgressions, he was crushed for our iniquities; the punishment that brought us peace was upon him, and by his wounds we are healed" (Is. 53:5). Thank God for the Passover and for the death and resurrection of Jesus which is the explanation for our communion service today.

Stand with the Minority

After Moses lead them through the Red Sea on dry ground, God commanded Moses to send twelve men to spy out the land of Canaan, a land flowing with milk and honey. When they returned and gave their report, ten men were afraid and persuaded the nation to rebel against Moses. In anger, God was destroying the people, but Moses interceded on their behalf. Because of their lack of faith, God punished the Israelites by sending them to wander in the wilderness for 40 years. (Numbers 13-14).

What New Ground Is God Asking You to Conquer?

Are we like Joshua and Caleb who had faith to believe God would give the enemy into their hands or are we like the ten spies who trembled in fear? Because of their lack of trusting God to take the land he was going to destroy them. Moses reminded God that the other nations of the world will scoff at him because he led them out of Egypt but couldn't deliver them to the land of Canaan. What new ground is God asking you to conquer? Claim his resurrection power and move ahead even though you may stand alone.

No Obedience Without Sacrifice

Moses chose to be mistreated along with the people of God rather than to enjoy the pleasures of sin for a short time. (Heb. 11:25-26). Are you double-minded? Jesus said that we cannot love both God and money. (Matt. 6:24). A double-minded person is unstable in all they do. (James 1:8). Are you laying aside the sensual pleasures of the ungodly culture so you can serve Jesus?

Moses chose mistreatment rather than the pleasures of this world. Jesus asks us to do the same. "Anyone who intends to come with me has to let me lead. You're not in the driver's seat; I am. Don't run from suffering; embrace it. Follow me and I'll show you how. Self-help is no help at all. Self-sacrifice is the way, my way, to finding yourself, your true self. What kind of deal is it to get everything you want but lose yourself? What would you ever trade your soul for?" (Matt. 16:24-26 Msg.). John reminds us we are not to love the world or the things in the world. (I John 2:15). The majority of the spies lacked faith, and as a consequence, died in the wilderness.

Motivation: Look Ahead

How could Moses choose the hard life rather than a life of ease? "He regarded disgrace for the sake of Christ as of greater value than the treasures of Egypt, because he was looking ahead to his reward." (Heb. 11:26). His secret was—looking ahead. He had faith and hope in the future. We are urged to look for Jesus' glorious appearing. (Titus. 2:13). Paul instructs Timothy: "You take over. I'm about to die, my life is an offering on God's altar. This is the only race worth running. I've run hard right to the finish, believing all the way. All that's left now is the shouting - God's applause! Depend on it, he's an honest judge. He'll do right not only by me, but by everyone eager for his coming" (II Tim. 4:7-8 Msg). Are you eager for his coming? Is your focus on earthly things or on God's eternal reward?

Paul admonishes the Colossians to "Set your hearts on things above, where Christ is, seated at the right hand of God. Set your minds on things above, not on earthly things" (Col. 3:1-2). "We always thank God for you.... We think of your faithful work, your loving deeds, and your continual anticipation of the return of our Lord Jesus Christ" (I Thess. 1:2-3 NLT). "May he strengthen your hearts so that you will be blameless, and holy in the presence of our God and Father when our Lord Jesus comes with all his holy ones" (I Thess. 3:13). (5:23-24). "You ought to live holy and godly lives as you look forward to the day of God and speed its coming... Dear friends, in keeping with his promise we are looking forward to this, make every effort to be found spotless, blameless and at peace with him" (II Peter 3:12-14).

When is the last time you heard a message on Jesus return? Moses looked ahead. Where is your focus?

JOSHUA

The Overcomer

HEBREWS 22:30

You Are Commissioned

Before Moses died he commissioned Joshua to take his place in leading the Israelites. (Numbers 27:22-23). Joshua was one of the twelve spies Moses sent to spy out the land of Canaan. He and Caleb were the only two of the twelve that gave a good report. Because of the lack of faith on the part of the other ten spies, the Children of Israel wandered forty "years in the wilderness."

The Lord told Joshua to be strong and courageous as he led the people across the Jordan River. "Go and possess the land I promised your forefathers." Joshua led the two million Israelites across the Jordan River at flood stage. (Joshua 3:14). God dramatically stopped the flow of water enabling all the Israelites to cross on dry land just as he performed the same miracle at the Red Sea years before. "He did this so that all the people of the earth might know that the hand of the Lord is powerful and so that you might always fear (and revere) the Lord your God." (4:24).

Learning from Past Experience

After crossing through the Jordan River, Joshua's first assignment was to appoint two men to spy out the land of Canaan. Years before when Moses sent the twelves spies only two were men of faith. Joshua, being one of the two faithful spies, learned from this experience the importance of finding men of faith. When the two spies returned they reported to Joshua, "The Lord has surely given the whole land into our hands; all the people are melting in fear because of us" (Josh. 2:24). Do you learn from your past experience? We say,

"Experience is the best teacher." That is not true for most people because too often we do not reflect or learn from our mistakes. Why do such a high percentage of prisoners return to prison? Ask God to give you wisdom so you don't keep repeating the same mistakes over and over. Move on to maturity. There is a Pennsylvania Dutch saying, "Too soon old, too late smart."

March Around the City

Jericho was the first city the Israelites encountered when they crossed the Jordan into Canaan. It was a small city with a circumference of 650 yards or about seven acres.[19] News of the Israelites crossing the rapid flowing of the Jordan River on dry ground spread quickly. The inhabitants of Jericho lived in fear as to what the God of the Israelites would do next. (5:1).

The commander of the Lord's army appeared to Joshua announcing victory for Israel's army if they obeyed his instructions. (Joshua 6). The instructions were to march around the city carrying the Ark of the Covenant which was the focus of God's presence and blessing. Each morning for six days, as the Israelites marched, their confidence grew. On the seventh day, as God instructed them, they marched around the city seven times. Then Joshua commanded the people "Shout! For the Lord has given you the city!" The walls collapsed and each man marched straight ahead conquering the city. (6:20).

Boldness Intimidates Our Enemies

"By faith the walls of Jericho fell, after the people had marched around them for seven days" (Heb. 11:30). Miracles are often a matter of timing. At just the perfect time God collapsed the wall.

Paul encourages the Christians at Philippi to be bold, "Don't be intimidated in any way by your enemies. This will be a sign to them that they are going to be destroyed, but that you are going to be saved, even by God himself" (Phil. 1:28-29 NLT). The same is true today as we hear of the boldness of persons who are persecuted

---

[19] (See the footnote, Joshua 7:25 in the Amplified Bible.)

and speak of their joy that surpasses the persecution. In the book, *Hearts of Fire* published by the Voice of the Martyrs, there are accounts of eight different women from eight different countries who suffered horrifically. Their testimony of God's grace and their boldness to return to the "streets" to share Jesus, even though risking their lives, challenges anyone who reads or hears about their experience.

Moses Commissioned Joshua

Just as Moses commissioned Joshua, we are commissioned by God. Jesus said in speaking to his Father, "Just as you sent me into the world, I am sending them into the world" (John 17:18 NLT; 20:21). Jesus final words to us: "I have been given all authority in heaven and on earth. Therefore, go and make disciples of all the nations, ... Teach these new disciples to obey all the commands I have given you" (Matt. 28:18-20 NLT). This commissioning is not just for leaders but for everyone. Have you taken Jesus' commission seriously?

Success Without a Successor Is Failure

Moses mentored Joshua to be his successor. Someone said, "Success without a successor is failure." So, few Christians are mentoring a successor. Who are you discipling or mentoring? Paul reminded Timothy to "Teach these great truths to trustworthy people who are able to pass them on to others" (II Tim. 2:2 NLT). Barnabas mentored Paul, Aquila and Priscilla mentored Apollos, Silas was a model for John Mark, Paul mentored Timothy and Titus. Today most Christians are more focused on salvation than mentoring or training disciples. That's one reason our churches have little influence in our degenerating culture. Disciples pass on their faith to the next generation because they live faithfully for Christ by what they say and do. Today, Christians in America are so independent that few are willing to be mentored. As this pattern continues, the churches' influence will continue to decline.

Faith and Obedience

Victory came to Joshua's men because of their obedience to follow the Lord's instruction. The word "obedience" appears 138 times in Scripture. Faith and obedience are couplets that must never be separate. Notice how Paul puts this couplet in Romans 1:5 NLT. "God has given us the privilege and authority to tell Gentiles everywhere what God has done for them, so that they will believe and obey him bringing glory to his name." Jesus said, "Not all people who sound religious (or who say they believe) are really godly. They may refer to me as 'Lord,' but they still won't enter the Kingdom of heaven. The decisive issue is whether they obey my Father in heaven'" (Matt. 7:22-23 NLT).

At the final judgment Jesus said, "The King will... say, 'Away with you, you cursed ones, into the eternal fire prepared for the Devil and his demons. For I was hungry and you didn't feed me. I was thirsty, and you didn't give me anything to drink. I was a stranger, and you didn't invite me into your home. I was naked, and you gave me no clothing. I was sick and in prison and you did not visit me. Then they will reply, 'Lord, when did we ever see you hungry or thirsty, or a stranger or naked or sick or in prison, and not help you?' And he will answer, 'I assure you when you refused to help the least of these my brothers and sisters you were refusing to help me. And they will go away into eternal punishment, but the righteous will go into eternal life." (Matt. 25:41-45 NLT).

Cheap Grace

Obedience is often overlooked today because we have come to accept cheap grace. Dietrich Bonhoeffer warned that cheap gracc is the deadly enemy of the Church. "Cheap grace is the preaching of forgiveness without requiring repentance, baptism without church discipline, communion without confession, absolution without personal confession. Cheap grace is grace without discipleship, grace without the cross, grace without Jesus Christ, living and incarnate." Bonhoeffer calls us to 'costly grace' which "is costly because it cost a man his life, and it is grace because it gives a man the only true life."

If a child says, I know mother will forgive me for making the floor dirty with my muddy shoes. That is disrespectful and rude. How often do we hear, "I know God will forgive me if I do what I know I should not be doing?" God is longsuffering and merciful, but deliberate disobedience grieves the Holy Spirit and cuts off the power flow from our life, leaving us barren and unfruitful. (Eph. 4:30).

Jesus explained: "A man had a fig tree growing in his vineyard, and he went to look for fruit but did not find any. So, he said to the man who took care of the vineyard, 'For three years I've been coming to look for fruit and haven't found any. Cut it down! Why should it use up the soil?' 'Sir,' 'the man replied, 'leave it alone for one more year, and I'll dig around it and fertilize it. If it bears fruit next year, fine! If not, then cut it down.'" (Luke 13:6-9). This tree was occupying good space and was producing nothing. Jesus warns his followers that God will not tolerate our deliberate disobedience and lack of productivity forever. There comes a time when deliberate disobedience cuts off God's patience. John the Baptist gave the same message: "An ax is ready to cut the trees down at their roots. Any tree that doesn't produce good fruit will be cut down and thrown into the fire" (Luke 3:9 TEV).

Obedience and Rewards

It is God who gives us the will and the power to obey him. "Be careful to put into action God's saving work in your lives, obeying God with deep reverence and fear. For God is working in you giving you the desire to obey him and the power to do what pleases him" (Phil. 2:12-13 NLT).

Obedience is not a burden. (I John 5:3). Pure love has a deep passion to please. Jesus said, "If you love me you will obey what I commanded" (John 14:15). If anyone loves me, he will obey my teaching" (John 14:23). It's a joy to have the privilege to obey our Lord and Father, the Almighty God of the cosmos.

Peter writes, "God's Spirit has made you holy. As a result, you have obeyed Jesus Christ and are cleansed by his blood.... Obey God because you are his children. Your heavenly Father... has no favorites when he judges" (I Peter 2, 14 and 17).

"The Lord will reward each for the good they do" (Eph. 6:8). God "will judge all people according to what they have done. He will give eternal life to those who persist in doing what is good, seeking after the glory and honor and immortality that God offers. But he will pour out his anger and wrath on those who live for themselves, who refuse to obey the truth and practice evil deeds" (Ro. 2:6 - 8 NLT). "I am coming soon, and my reward is with me, to repay all according to their deeds" (Rev. 22:12).

Choose Well Your Path

Solomon started out well, but he was led astray by his many foreign wives. On the other hand, Joshua ended well. "Israel served the Lord through the lifetime of Joshua." (Joshua 24:31). After leading the nation for more than fifty years Joshua gives his extended farewell address in which he challenges his people: "Fear the Lord and serve him with all faithfulness. Throw away the gods your forefathers worshiped beyond the River and in Egypt, and serve the Lord... But as for me and my household, we will serve the Lord" (Joshua 24:14-15).

RAHAB

From Harlot to God's Hall of Faith

HEBREWS 11:31

"[Prompted] by faith Rahab the prostitute was not destroyed along with those who refused to believe and obey, because she had received the spies in peace (without enmity)" (Heb. 11:31 AMP).

Soon after the Israelites crossed the Jordan River, Joshua sent two spies to check out the land God promised them. (Joshua 2:1). The King of Jericho learned that the spies were in his country and believed they were in the home of Rahab, the prostitute. Her house, located in the city wall of Jericho, was likely an inn as well as a brothel. Its location was an excellent place for the spies to hide, since it made it relatively easy for the spies to escape.

In many countries where it is "illegal" to be a Christian, God delivers people on a daily basis while others suffer torture and death. I know a missionary friend and his wife, who while sharing their Christian faith by God's grace, managed to escape the authorities. In our faith Chapter, Paul, after listing many who escaped writes: "Others were tortured and refused to be released, so that they might gain a better resurrection. Some faced jeers and floggings, while still others were chained and put in prison. They were stoned; they were sawed in two; they were put to death by the sword. They went about in sheepskins and goatskins, destitute, persecuted and mistreated" (Heb. 11:35-38).

At the Bottom

Rahab, the harlot, was at the bottom of the social ladder. God frequently uses persons our society rejects to carry out his plans. Jesus said, "I tell you, the tax collectors and the prostitutes are entering the kingdom of God ahead of you" (Matt. 21:31). Today the child sex abusers, those selling drugs, the drug lords, the jihad rulers, the terrorists and dictators are among those who are despised and feared. Remember Paul's conversion—from persecutor to missionary for Jesus. Although Madalyn Murry O'Hair removed audible prayer and bible reading in public schools and founded an atheist organization, her son, Bill, is a devout Christian leader.

Today I texted a man who is angry at God for not giving him what he wants. He is fighting depression and is suicidal. Although he is at the bottom of the social ladder, God can transform his life just as he did for demoniac and the demon possessed girl at Philippi. Who are the Rahabs in your community? Do you believe they can become new creations in Christ Jesus? Do you pray and relate to them?

Rahab Feared God

Rahab heard reports of how Israel's God miraculously delivered his people. She had an unquestioning belief that Israel's God was going to deliver Jericho into their hands. She knew the city of Jericho was living in great fear knowing what God had done elsewhere. She also knew the Israelites greatly outnumbered those in Jericho.

Even though the people in Jericho believed they were about to be conquered by Israel's God, they did not pray for deliverance. They feared God but had no faith in God. James says that the devil believes in God and trembles but of course the devil gives no allegiance to God. (James 2:19). Multitudes today have a head knowledge of God but have no intention of giving their allegiance to him.

Take "Risks" for God

When the spies came to her house, Rahab perceived immediately that these men were not Amorites but spies from Israel. She risked her life by welcoming and providing protection under the flax that was drying on the flat roof of her house. This proved to be an excellent hiding place for the spies.

"Before the spies lay down for the night, she went up on the roof and said to them, 'I know that the Lord has given you this land and that a great fear of you has fallen on us, so that all who live in this country are melting in fear because of you. We have heard how the Lord dried up the water of the Red Sea for you when you came out of Egypt, and what you did to Sihon and Og, the two kings of the Amorites... whom you completely destroyed. When we heard of it, our hearts melted in fear and everyone's courage failed because of you, for the Lord your God is God in heaven above and on the earth below. Now then, please swear to me by the Lord that you will show kindness to my family because I have shown kindness to you. Give me a sure sign that you will spare the lives of my father and mother, my brothers and sisters, and all who belong to them—and that you will save us from death" (Josh. 2:8-13).

The King heard about the spies and sent messengers to apprehend them. If they found the spies, Rahab would be guilty of treason and both she and the spies would have received the death sentence. When the king's messengers came, Rahab deceived them and sent them outside the city to search for the spies. (For deception in the Old Testament see the section: "Abraham Stumbles" in the chapter on Abraham.)

The spies agreed to spare Rahab and her family provided she hung a scarlet cord out of the window, for the house she lived in was part of the city wall. Using the cord, she lowered them to the ground and sent them into a mountainous terrain in the opposite direction the King's messengers had gone. That scarlet cord likely because of its color helped to remind the Israelites of the Passover in Egypt which many believe foretells the sacrificial work of Christ. (Exodus 12:13 and Heb. 9:22).

Redemption

Rahab became the wife of Salmon, one of the two spies she sheltered. Salmon was a leader of the kingly tribe of Judah which meant that Rahab married into one of the most important families of Israel. She became the mother of Boaz. Two generations later King David was born. Eventually through David's posterity Jesus was born of the Virgin Mary. (Matt. 1:5).

Do you feel you could never be part of God's Hall of Faith because of your family background or sinful lifestyle? God can use anyone. We are all sinners. There is no one righteous, not even one... there is no one who seeks God. (Rom. 3:10). Lift up your head and thank God for what he has done for you, not because you are good but because he loves you and longs for your allegiance. Rahab is included in God's Hall of Faith to encourage us when we think we are too sinful for God to redeem.

Forgiveness and Deliverance

While operating a brothel had possibly estranged her from her loved ones, Rahab was concerned about their safety as well as her own. What a picture of forgiving love. Have you forgiven family members and relatives of past sins? Multitudes have been abused physically, verbally and sexually. God will bring healing to you if you earnestly surrender your pain and hurt to him. For many, healing will not happen instantly but over time. Rahab wanted the kindness she was shown to include her entire family.

After the spies reported their finding to Joshua, he instructed them to go into the Rahab's house and bring her and all who belonged to her to safety in accordance with the oath they had given to her. Then they burned the whole city and everything in it. Joshua spared Rahab with her family because she hid the men Joshua had sent as spies to Jericho. (Joshua 6:22-25).

GIDEON

Destroyer of Evil

HEBREWS 11:32

Paul realized he could not list all those who are in God's Hall of Fame. He wrote: "It would take too long to recount the stories of the faith of Gideon, Barak, Samson, Jephthah, David, Samuel, and all the prophets" (Heb. 11:32 NLT). Therefore, he mentioned some of their trials and victories and began chapter 12, "Since we are surrounded by such a great cloud of witnesses, (those listed in chapter 11 and all who have died in Christ since then), let us throw off everything that hinders and the sin that so easily entangles, and let us run with perseverance the race marked out for us. Let us fix our eyes on Jesus... who for the joy set before him endured the cross, scorning its shame, and sat down at the right hand of the throne of God. Consider him who endured such opposition from sinful men, so that you will not grow weary and lose heart." (12:1-3 AMP.).

After Joshua, "The Israelites did evil in the eyes of the Lord. For seven years he gave them into the hands of the Midianites. Midian was so cruel, the Israelites prepared shelters for themselves in mountain clefts, caves and strongholds. Whenever the Israelites planted their crops, the Midianites, Amalekites and other eastern peoples invaded the country. They camped on the land and ruined the crops... Midian so impoverished the Israelites they cried out to the Lord for help" (Judges 6:1-6).

A Vicious Cycle

Following Joshua's farewell address the nation drifted further and further from God. Over the next 325 years, (1325—1000 BC), God raised up 12 judges. Gideon was the sixth judge. The Israelites were caught in a vicious cycle. The judges delivered the Israelites calling them back in allegiance to God. However, in a few years, they soon returned to serving the gods of the nations around them, until finally, everyone did what was right in their own eyes. (17:6). "The Israelites did evil in the sight of the Lord" is a phrase used 100 times in the books of Judges, Kings and Chronicles. The fact that God didn't wipe them out, as he did many other nations, shows his incredible mercy.

Why didn't they cry out to the Lord before they were so ravished? Their pride blocked them from humbling themselves to admit their need for God's help. We are no better. God makes himself known to us if we have our minds and hearts open to him. He speaks through his Word, through prophets, through creation, through our conscience, through other people and even though miracles. But if we are blinded by our self-centered nature, we cannot recognize his voice.

Since the heart of mankind is the same, whether in the time of the judges, the time of Rome or today, Paul mirrored humanity with these words: "Because you are stubborn and refuse to turn from your sin, you are storing up terrible punishment for yourself. A day of anger is coming, when God's righteous judgment will be revealed" (Rom. 2:5 NLT). "The god of this age has blinded the minds of unbelievers, so that they cannot see the light of the gospel of the glory of Christ" (II Cor. 4:4). "Their minds were made dull, for to this day the same veil remains when the old covenant is read. It has not been removed, because only in Christ is it taken away" (II Cor. 3:14). Paul explained to Timothy, "They will turn their ears away from the truth and turn aside to myths" (I Tim. 4:4).

We fail to heed Isaiah's admonition: "Lift your eyes and look at the heavens: Who created all these? He brings out the starry host one by one, and calls them each by name" (Is. 40:26). David reminds us, "The heavens declare the glory of God; the skies proclaim the work of his hands. Day after day they pour forth speech; night after night they display knowledge. There is no speech or language where their voice is not heard. Their voice goes out into all the earth, their words to the ends of the world" (Ps. 19:1-4).

Since God's creation points us to his power and divinity, we are responsible to give him allegiance. Paul's description of humanity is relevant for every age: "The wrath of God is being revealed from heaven against all the godlessness and wickedness of men who suppress the truth by their wickedness, since what may be known about God is plain to them, because God has made it plain to them. For since the creation of the world God's invisible qualities—his eternal power and divine nature—have been clearly seen, being understood from what has been made, so that men are without excuse. For although they knew God, they neither glorified him as God nor gave thanks to him, but their thinking became futile and their foolish hearts were darkened. They claimed to be wise; they became fools and exchanged the glory of the immortal God for images made to look like mortal man and birds and animals and reptiles. Therefore, God gave them over in the sinful desires of their heart to sexual impurity for the degrading of their bodies with one another. They exchanged the truth of God for a lie, and worshipped and served created things rather than the Creator" (Rom. 1:18-25).

Reading Paul's words may cause us to say we are not nearly as evil as those people he is describing. However, let me paint a picture of what is happening all around us.

The Spirit World, Satan Worship

Nick Pitts in his daily blog reports a statement from the police that, "Florida middle school girls plotted to kill up to 15 students and drink their blood. (Fox News, h/t: Will M)" He continues: "Two middle school students in Florida were arrested after they concocted a 'plot to kill students' via a variety of weapons, including a pizza cutter." Police said. "The girls—ages 11 and 12 years old—'wanted to kill at least 15 people,' Bartown Police Chief Joe Hall said at a news conference Wednesday: The two, were waiting in the bathroom for (an) opportunity to find smaller kids that they could overpower to be their victims. The girls admitted to investigators that they were "Satan-worshippers." The girls, all claimed, 'they were willing to drink blood, and possibly eat flesh.'"[20]

Today many of the images especially on children's products are depicting violence. This reminds me of Paul's letter to the Romans where he says people claim to be wise but they become fools and

---

[20] Nick Pitts, Oct. 25, 2018 daily blog. He serves as the Executive Director of the Institute for Global Engagement at Dallas Baptist University.

exchange the glory of God for images made to look like mortal man, birds, animals and reptiles. Weeks prior to Halloween various houses already display ghosts, witches, grotesque reptiles, skeletons rising out of caskets. Spiders and spider webs draped from second story windows. Other images clearly suggest immoral sexual overtures.

History of Halloween

"The American Halloween tradition of "trick-or-treating" probably dates back to the All Souls' Day in England. During the festivities, poor citizens would beg for food. Families would give them pastries called "soul cakes" for their promise to pray for the family's dead relatives...

"On Halloween, when it was believed that ghosts came back to the earthly world, people thought that they would encounter ghosts if they left their homes. To avoid being recognized by these ghosts, people would wear masks when they left their homes after dark so that the ghosts would mistake them for fellow spirits. On Halloween, to keep ghosts away from their houses, people would place bowls of food outside their homes to appease the ghosts and prevent them from attempting to enter... Halloween has always been a holiday filled with mystery, magic and superstition. It began as a Celtic festival during which people felt especially close to deceased relatives and friends...

"Today's Halloween ghosts are often depicted as more fearsome. Our customs and superstitions are scarier too. We avoid crossing paths with black cats, afraid that they might bring us bad luck. This idea has its roots in the Middle Ages, when many people believed that witches avoided detection by turning themselves into black cats... Other rituals include helping young women to identify their future husband... Fortune-tellers help people avoid seven years of bad luck. These superstations depend on the "spirit" world for their powers."[21]

Many major cities in the U.S. have cultic clubs where the participants learn to cast spells and empower evil spirits. "Seventy three

---

[21] These three paragraphs are from https://history.com/topical/halloween/history-of-halloween#section_1.

percent of youth have participated in at least one type of psychic or witchcraft related activity."[22]

Moses and many of the prophets warned the people to abstain from witchcraft. "When you enter the land the Lord your God is given you, do not learn to imitate the detestable ways of the nations there. Let no one be found among you who sacrifices his son or daughter in the fire, who practices divination or sorcery, interprets omens, engages in witchcraft, or cast spells, or who is a medium or spiritist or who consults the dead. Anyone who does these things is detestable to the Lord and because of these detestable practices the Lord your God will drive out those nations before you" (Deut. 18:9-13 NLT).

In speaking of his return Jesus says, "Outside (the city) are... those who practice magic arts, the sexually immoral, the murderers, the idolaters..." (Rev. 22:15 NLT).

Do these Halloween customs and traditions bring you closer to Jesus? Might they open the door for fascination with the spirit world? Would Jesus celebrate Halloween rituals? Paul's admonition takes on new relevance: "Put on the full armor of God so that you can take your stand against the devil's schemes. For our struggle is not against flesh and blood, but against the rulers, against the authorities, against the power of the dark world and against the spiritual forces of evil in the heavenly realms" (Eph. 6:11-12).

God Speaks Today

Prior to Gideon, the Israelites experienced an unusual time of victory under Deborah's leadership. Forgetting how God had delivered them they must endure the consequences of being ravished by the nations around them. Today, just like the Israelites of Gideon's day, many people have a superficial relationship with God. More than half of those who call themselves Christians believe that all the major religions pray to the same God. We spend two hours a day watching TV and another hour on our iPhones. More than fifty million people in the U.S. play violent video games an hour or more a day.

---

[22] (www.crosswalk.com/special-coverage/halloween).

God has given us a conscience. "The true light coming into the world—the genuine, perfect, steadfast Light—that illumines every person..." (John 1:9 Amp.). When people deny God long enough, their conscience is seared. (I Tim. 4:2). We all know it is wrong to push grandma into the path of an oncoming train. We know it is wrong to kill innocent people, especially children. We are born with a desire for justice and righteousness because we are born in the image of God. (Gen. 1:27). His stamp is on every heart, but multitudes ignore it.

There Is a Remedy

Jesus understands our dilemma and will come to rescue us if we humble ourselves and call to him. "When outsiders, who have never heard of God's law, follow it more or less by instinct, they confirm its truth by their obedience. They show that God's law is... woven into the very fabric of our creation. There is something deep within them that echoes God's yes and no, right and wrong." (Ro. 2:14-15 Msg.).

How can we be saved? "We are not godly. We are constant sinners so your anger is heavy on us... We are all infected and impure with sin. When we proudly display our righteous deeds, we find they are but filthy rags... Yet no one calls on your name or pleads with you for mercy. Therefore, you have turned away from us and turned us over to our sins" (Isaiah 64:5b-7 NLT).

God Calls Gideon

After being ravished by the Midianites for seven years, God's people finally call on God to deliver them. (Judges 6:1-6). Gideon is in hiding in a winepress for fear of the Midianites. The angel of the Lord appears to Gideon, "The Lord is with you, mighty warrior" (6:12). Gideon responds, "If that is true why are we in this position?" The Lord said to him, "Go in the strength you have and save Israel out of Midian's hand. Am I not sending you?" (v.14). God says to us, "Use the strength I have given you."

Gideon makes excuses. "My clan is the weakest... and I am the least of my family." At this the Lord promised he would be with him. (Judges 6:15-16). Gideon hesitated and asked for a sign to buttress his faith. God told him to demolish the altars of the god Baal. He demolished them at night because he was afraid of his people.

The enemy joined forces and camped in the valley of Jezreel. Gideon said to God, "I will place a wool fleece on the threshing floor. If there is dew only on the fleece and all the ground is dry then I'll know you will save Israel." He still was not satisfied and asked God to let the fleece be dry and all the ground wet with dew and God did so. (6:36-40).

Asking God for a sign is an indication of our lack of faith. As we mature and learn to walk in a more intimate relationship with Jesus, experiencing his leading daily, we will find less need for a sign. Jesus said to the Pharisees: "You know how to interpret the appearance of the sky, but you cannot interpret the signs of the times. A wicked and adulterous generation looks for a sign, but none will be given it except the sign of Jonah." (Matt. 16:3-4). We have the most potent sign: Jesus' death and resurrection and his Spirit living in us. What more can we ask for?

The Pharisees and Sadducees saw Jesus preform many miracles, but they would not believe. The rich man in Luke 16 wanted Abraham to warn his brothers, so they would not have to come to this place of torment. Abraham reminds the rich man that they have Moses and the prophets. The rich man replied, "'No' Father Abraham! But if someone is sent to them from the dead, they will turn from their sins.' But Abraham said, 'If they won't listen to Moses and the prophets, they won't listen even if someone rises from the dead'" (vv.27-31 NLT). Miracles are everywhere if we have eyes and hearts to see them.

God Proves Himself Again

Israel prepared for battle with the Midianites. (Judges 7). Gideon rounded up his army but the Lord informed him his army was too large. A large army would boast that they won the battle in their own strength. Gideon announced: "anyone who trembles with fear may turn back and leave... twenty-two thousand left and ten thousand remained." "The Lord told Gideon there are still too many. 'Take them down to the spring. Watch how each man gets a drink... Then divide them into two groups—those who lap the water like a dog and those who kneel down to drink.'" This reduced the army to three hundred. Gideon was afraid of the huge army of Midianites. God told him to go to the Midianite camp and listen. There he was encouraged when he heard the interpretation of a dream that clearly pictured the destruction of the Midianites. (Judges 7:13-14).

The 300 men surrounded the camp. At Gideon's signal they blew their trumpets and shouted, "A sword for the Lord, and for Gideon." (7:20). The Lord caused the Midianite men to turn on each other with their swords. (7:22). The 300 never used their swords. God was teaching the Israelites that victory comes from him, not from the strength of their military.

What Is God trying to Teach America Today?

No nation has stood more than a few hundred years. "From one-man God made every nation of men, that they should inhabit the whole earth; and he determined the times set for them and the exact places where they should live" (Acts 17:26). Isaiah reminds us, "The nation that will not serve you will perish; it will be utterly ruined" (60:12). This is why we are urged to pray for all those in authority. (I Tim. 2:1-2). God has no grandchildren. This means we must teach the next generation the ways of the Lord or our nation will be destroyed.

Jesus promised he will be with us in life or in death. He warns that all men will hate us. (Matt. 10:22). We are not to fear men who can kill the body but fear God who can cast body and soul into hell. (Matt. 10:28). The early Christians focused on their future city. They "Joyfully accepted the confiscation of their property, because they knew they had better and lasting possessions." (Heb.10:34). Christians are persecuted in 144 countries of our world. Pray for the Lord to enable us to be faithful in persecution.

The Greatest Miracle Is a Transformed Life

The greatest miracle is the transformed life. Many persons are delivered from drug addiction, alcohol, hatred, jealousy, and despair. They find peace, joy and the power of the resurrected Christ. Invite people to experience this new life in Christ. (I Cor. 5:17).

As a stuttering youth and young man, I was anxious about being a pastor. How could I be a pastor if I can't talk properly? A church asked me to be a candidate. What I discovered was that their current pastor had a definite speech impediment. To me this was an obvious sign to accept their invitation. Our son, Chet, was a missionary in South America. God spoke to him to go a certain place in Ohio and plant a church. He had no intention of doing such a thing but three days later he received a call from a group of pastors in that same community who were praying for a church planter and felt led to contact him.

Good Warrior But Poor Leader

Gideon became a passionate warrior. He humbled himself when they asked him to "rule over them." He pointed them to God. But he failed the test of a good leader when he requested their gold earrings and made an ephod, (a sacred, high priest's garment), which he displayed in his hometown. "All Israel prostituted themselves by worshiping this ephod and it became a snare to Gideon and his family." (Judges 8:22-28). It's so easy for us to be caught up in our position of honor as God uses us to spread his Kingdom. Don't neglect the need for an intimate relationship with God. Jesus said, "Apart from me, you can do nothing" (John 15:5). God says to us, "It is not by might, or by power, but by my Spirit, says the Lord Almighty" (Zech. 4:6).

BARAK

Overcomers Together

HEBREWS 11:32 | JUDGES 4 & 5

Barak was one of those mighty Hebrew warriors who answered the call of God despite overwhelming odds. His name means "lightning." The prophetess, Deborah, sent for Barak and said to him "The Lord, the God of Israel, commands you: Go, take with you ten thousand men of Naphtali and Zebulun and lead the way to Mount Tabor. I will lure Sisera, the commander of Jabin's army, with his chariots and his troops, to the Kishon River and give him into your hands." Barak said, "If you go with me, I will go; but if you don't go with me, I won't go" (Judges 4:6-9). Deborah agreed. She told Barak because of his lack of faith in God, the credit for this victory would not go to him but to a woman.

God had clearly instructed the Israelites to drive out the Canaanites from their land. Because they disobeyed God the people suffered greatly. Finally, after twenty years of repression by the Canaanites, the Israelites cried out to God for mercy. (Judges 4:2-3).

Why did they wait so long for God's help? Too often we are like the Israelites in waiting until the problem escalates rather than coming to God when we first realize there is a problem. We know in our heart what we should do, but we lack confidence to move ahead.

Ask for Help

Barak needed confidence and support. Eliciting the support of others is different from asking them to help us discern God's will when we already know his will. Asking for support in doing what God designed for us is one way to buttress our faith so we have confidence and boldness in carrying out God's will. Jesus sent the disciples out two-by-two, so they could support one another to carry out his commission.

"Two are better than one... If one falls, his friend can help him up, but pity the man who falls and has no one to help him up!... Though one may be overpowered, two can defend themselves. A cord of three strands is not quickly broken" (Ecclesiastes 4:9-12).

Barak Recognized the Enemy

It was clear to Barak that the Canaanites were far superior in strength. Israel's army was no match for the Canaanites who had 900 iron chariots. Many of the chariots had sharp knives extended from their wheels to mutilate foot soldiers. These chariots were like tanks: swift, intimidating and deadly.

Recognize your enemy. One of Satan's most effective tools is to have people think he does not exist. Today, most people including some Christians, do not recognize Satan as their enemy. Satan disguises himself as an angel of light deceiving us. (II Cor. 11:14). At other times, the devil prowls around like a roaring lion looking for someone to devour. We must resist him. "No test or temptation that comes your way is beyond the course of what others have had to face... remember, God will never let you be pushed past your limit; he'll always be there to help you come through it" (I Cor. 10:13 Msg.). We take courage because our brothers and sisters all throughout the world are experiencing similar suffering. (I Pet. 5:8-9).

Paul faced severe persecution and advised the Ephesians to: "Be strong in the Lord and in his mighty power. Put on the full armor of God so that you will be able to stand firm against all strategies of the devil. For we are not fighting against flesh-and-blood enemies, but against evil rulers and authorities of the unseen world, against mighty powers in this dark world, and against evil spirits in the heavenly places. (Eph. 6:10-12). The good news is that God's Spirit is in us and is more powerful than Satan who is the ruler of this present evil world. (I John 4:4, John 12:31).

Advance

Deborah told Barak to advance because the "Lord has gone before you." God created a massive rainstorm. The ground turned to mud, bogging down Sisera's chariots. The Kishon stream overflowed sweeping away many of the Canaanites. Barak and his men pursued those left behind until not one of Israel's enemies remained.

Be Sure Your Enemy Is Defeated

Although Israel's enemies were destroyed, Sisera, commander of the Canaanite army, managed to escape to the house of Jael. "She went out to meet Sisera and said to him, 'Come, my lord, come right in. Don't be afraid.' So, he entered her tent, and she put a covering over him. 'I'm thirsty,' he said. 'Please give me some water.' She opened a skin of milk, gave him a drink, and covered him up. 'Stand in the doorway of the tent,' he told her. 'If someone comes by and asks you, 'Is any one here?' say 'No.'" (4:18-20). Sisera was exhausted and fell asleep. While he was asleep she quietly took a tent peg and a hammer and drove the peg through Sisera's temple, killing him. (4:21). "Barak came by in pursuit of Sisera, and Jael went out to meet him. 'Come,' she said 'I will show you the man you're looking for.' So, he went in with her, and there lay Sisera with the tent peg through his temple—dead'" (4:22).

God subdued the Canaanites as the Israelites grew stronger and stronger. There was peace in Israel for 40 years. (5:31).

Barak's Immature Faith

When Barak requested Deborah's help, he was putting his faith in Deborah rather than in God. While Barak's faith was weak, his faith grew knowing Deborah was by his side. Do you put your faith in a godly man or woman rather than in God? Many put their faith in their godly parents, their pastor, or a close friend whom they trust rather than in God. Be sure your faith is in God alone. However, it is important for us to encourage each other in our faith journey. As Paul comes to the end of his life he says, "Fight the good fight of faith." (I Tim. 6:12).

We are never alone. "Since we are surrounded by such a great cloud of witnesses, let us throw off everything that hinders and the sin that so easily entangles, and let us run with perseverance the race marked out for us. Let us fix our eyes on Jesus.... Who, for the joy set before him, endured the cross, scorning its shame, and sat down at the right hand of God. Consider him who endured such opposition from sinful men so that you will not grow weary and lose heart (faith)" (Heb. 12:1-3).

Faith and Action

Barak put his faith in action. "Faith by itself, if it is not accompanied by action, is dead.... " (James 1:17, 22). Faith is like a muscle, exercise it and it will grow stronger. Peter informs us how to exercise our muscle of faith: Make every effort to add to your faith goodness, knowledge, self-control, perseverance, godliness, brotherly kindness and love. For if you possess these qualities in increasing measure, they will keep you from being ineffective and unproductive... (II Peter 1:5-8).

Live in God's Word and your faith will grow. "Faith comes from listening to this message of good news—the Good News about Christ" (Rom. 10:17 NLT). "Let your roots grow down into him and draw up nourishment from him, so you will grow in faith, strong and vigorous in the truth you were taught. Let your lives overflow with thanksgiving for all he has done" (Col. 2:7 NLT).

God Uses Who He Wishes

Barak recognized Deborah's authority came from God. He obeyed a woman - something rare in ancient times. Throughout the Hall of Faith, it is obvious that God uses anyone he chooses. Be careful not to put God in a box. He will use women like Deborah, and he will use an unknown man like Barak. He will use you!

SAMSON

What Could Have Been

HEB. 11:32 & JUDGES 13-16

Open Arms But Given a Cold Shoulder

The vicious cycle of oppression and deliverance of the Israelites continues. Because they insisted on serving other gods, they brought suffering and death upon themselves. In their stubbornness they chose not to come to God in repentance. God is love. He says, "All day long I have held out my hands to a disobedient and obstinate people" (Isaiah 65:2). God uses both goodness and judgment, but few turn to him in faith.

Paul writes: "You surely don't think much of God's wonderful goodness or of his patience and willingness to put up with you. Don't you know that the reason God is good to you is because he wants you to turn to him?" (Rom. 2:4 CEV). God's goodness is everywhere if our heart is open to see it: e.g. the beauty of his creation—the clouds, the flowers, trees, birds, etc.; the ability to think, talk, to show love; the ability to enjoy food and fellowship. There is no end to God's goodness. We know about God but we do not honor or thank him so he lets us go our own way to destruction. (Rom. 1:18-32). You would think we would cry out for his mercy and follow his leading.

You Are Chosen

"Again, the Israelites did evil in the eyes of the Lord, so the Lord delivered them into the hands of the Philistines for forty years" (Judges 13:1). God saw their suffering. He chose Samson, even before he was born, to deliver his people. (v. 3). "God chose us... before the creation of the world to be holy and blameless in his sight"

(Eph. 1:4). You are no afterthought with God. God made no mistake when he created you.

Samson's Unique Gift of Strength

Samson was a Nazirite from birth. He was never to cut his hair or drink wine. As long as he submitted to these restrictions he was capable of heroic achievements against the Philistines. Twelve different encounters are enumerated for us in Judges 13-15. Samson killed a lion with his bare hands, caught 300 foxes and tied torches on them and sent them through the fields burning the crops of the Philistines. He killed 1,000 Philistines with a donkey's jawbone and was so thirsty he cried out to God. God granted his request and miraculously brought water out of the ground to quench his thirst. (Judges 15:15-19). Another time Samson went to Gaza and saw a prostitute. People reported Samson was there, and they waited till dawn to capture and kill him. However, during the middle of the night, Samson escaped by taking the doors and the two posts of the city gate, tore them loose and carried them to the top of the hill in defiance of his enemy. (16:3).

A Proud Man

Samson had tremendous potential. He was born to free his people from the Philistines. He was given great strength, but he wasted his strength on practical jokes against the Philistines. He tried to satisfy Delilah the Philistine woman he loved. "The rulers of the Philistines went to her and said, 'See if you can lure him into showing you the secret of his great strength and how we can overpower him so we can tie him up and subdue him. Each one of us will give you eleven hundred shackles of silver" (Judges 16:5).

Delilah nagged him for seven days until he finally succumbed and told her the secret of his tremendous strength was his Nazarite vow. She lured him to sleep. They promptly cut off his hair draining his strength. The Philistines gouged out his eyes, put him in prison and made him a slave to turn the grinding rock like an ox. Here he had time to think and repent. As his hair grew, his strength returned. At a Philistine celebration in the temple of their god, Dagon, they called

Samson out of prison to entertain them. He asked his attendant to lead him to the two large pillars supporting the temple. He prayed: "O Sovereign Lord, remember me, O God, please strengthen me just once more, and let me with one blow get revenge on the Philistines for my two eyes" (16:28). He pushed with all his might and down came the temple, killing the rulers and all the people in it. "He killed many more while he died, than while he lived" (v. 30). Samson's prayer expresses his genuine faith as he addresses the Lord as Sovereign, God above all gods. For that he is included in God's Hall of Faith.

Temptation

The lure of sexual temptations was greater than Samson's physical strength. He deceived himself when he saw a prostitute and slept with her. Later he fell in love with Delilah who deceived him into revealing his true source of strength. Today, multitudes of men and women are defeated by sexual temptations. Don't be deceived. In the New Testament most of the 17 catalogues of sin begin with sexual immorality. Pornography for both men and women has become an epidemic resulting in the collapse of an unbelievable number of homes. It is the most prominent sin found in our churches. How can we be so foolish? Job said, "I made a covenant with my eyes not to look with lust upon a young woman." (Job 31:1, NLT). The Holy Spirit will give us victory, so we can bring every thought into submission to Jesus Christ. (II Cor. 10:5).

What Is Your Gift?

Samson had a gift of unusual strength. There are thirty-some specific gifts listed in the bible. As followers of Jesus you have several gifts. Don't ever think that God has skipped you when he passed out gifts. (Eph. 4:7-8). Everyone is unique, which means your gifts are expressed differently from everyone else. "There are different kinds of spiritual gifts, but they all come from the same Spirit. There are different ways to serve the same Lord, and we can each do different things. Yet the same God works in all of us and helps us in everything we do. The Spirit has given each of us a special way of serving others" (I Cor. 12:4-7 CEV). (See also Rom. 12:6-8; I Pet. 4:10-11).

Wasted Potential

We see Samson's wasted potential. He could have strengthened his nation. He could have returned his people to the worship of God. He could have wiped out the Philistines. But even though he did none of these things, Samson still accomplished the purpose announced by the angel who visited his parents before his birth. He took the lead in rescuing Israel from the Philistines.

Use Your Gift

In Matthew 25, Jesus gives the parable of the talents. To one he gave ten, to another two and to another one. The first two invested their talents and gained much. The one who "had received the one talent said, 'Master, I knew you to be a hard man, harvesting where you did not sow, and gathering where you scattered no seed. So, I was afraid, and went out and hid your talent in the ground...' His master replied, 'You wicked and lazy servant!... you ought to have put my money with the bankers... Take the talent from him and give it to him who has the ten talents. For everyone who has will be given more.... whoever does not have, even what they have will be taken from them. And throw that worthless servant outside, in to the darkness, where there will be weeping and gnashing of teeth." (Matt. 25:24 - 30).

It's clear if you do not use your gifts you not only hurt yourself, you are making it more difficult for others to become disciples of Christ.

Our Amazing God

Our amazing God loved and forgave Samson using him to defeat the wicked Philistines. Don't ever say you are beyond God's grace. He forgave Samson, and he will forgive you and use you. We learn from Samson's example that it is never too late to start over. We need a heart change, showing remorse for wasting God's gifts. God will forgive and redeem us as we put our complete trust in him.

JEPHTHAH

Outcast

HEB. 11:32 | JUDGES 11:1-12:7

"Jephthah, the Gilalite was a mighty warrior. His father was Gilead; his mother was a prostitute. Gilead's wife also bore him sons. When they were grown, they drove Jephthah away. 'You are not going to get any inheritance in our family,' they said, 'because you are the son of another woman.' So, Jephthah fled form his brothers and settled...in Tub, where a gang of scoundrels gathered around him and followed him." (Judges 11:1-3).

Blended or Stepfamilies

Many can identify with Jephthah. Through no fault of your own you inherit new parents along with new siblings. In most every blended family it's common for jealousy and envy to raise its ugly head.

Mary T. Kelly, M.A. on Twitter: www.twitter.com/mwbaggage gives the following perspective. "The traditional Mom and Dad in the house raising the kids no longer represents the majority of families in the U.S. As of 2014, the majority of families are made up of stepfamilies, singles and families living together outside of marriage. Two out of three people have a step-relative. Forty percent of married couples with children are step couples. The divorce rate among remarriages that involve children is 62-74 percent. It's not easy to be in a stepfamily, whether you're the kid that has to go back and forth between two homes, the parents who have to split their parenting time 50/50, or the stepparent who comes in to a ready-made system."

God's Design for Marriage

God's design is for marriage to be between one man and one woman for life. Whenever we break that standard we live with the pain and trauma of broken relationships. Healing can happen, but usually it takes years for these relationships to become healthy. These family feuds overload courts and overflow our prisons. Determine by God's grace to put Jesus' standard above the worldly secular culture and avoid much of the pain and suffering of these broken relationships.

Although Jephthah suffered from the way his family treated him, God used his life. If you are suffering from rejection, remember, God used Jephthah and he can use you. Look around you and spot persons who are rejected by their family, by the church or their community. What would God have you do to encourage and help them, so they feel a sense of belonging?

The Ammonites Invade Gilead

"Sometime later, when the Ammonites made war on Israel, the elders of Gilead went to get Jephthah from the land of Tob. 'Come,' they said, 'be our commander so we can fight the Ammonites.' Jephthah said, 'Didn't you hate me and drive me from my father's house? Why do you come to me now, when you're in trouble?' The elders said, 'Nevertheless, we're turning to you now; come with us to fight the Ammonites, and you will be head over all who live in Gilead.'" (Judges 11:4-8).

It's remarkable that Jephthah even considered helping his people after they drove him away. Jephthah said, "Suppose you take me back to fight the Ammonites and the Lord gives them to me - will I really be your head?" He recognized it was the Lord who would give him the victory. Jephthah's faith is remarkable.

Jephthah's first move was to negotiate with the Ammonites. Jephthah was wise in not rushing into this tense situation. He made a serious effort to negotiate with the king of Ammon. (Judges 11:12-28). Talking things through and listening to the other side of any disagreement is much better than holding a grudge or taking revenge. After being sure his half-brothers were sincere, Jephthah sent messengers to the Ammonite king asking him, "What do you have against us that you have attacked our country?" The Ammonites falsely claimed that Israel took land from them. (vv. 12-13). Jephthah gave a long explanation explaining that their claim was not true. But the king of Ammon paid no attention to his message.

The Spirit of the Lord came on Jephthah and the Lord gave them into his hands. He devastated twenty towns. The Ammonites were subdued. (vv. 29-33).

Take the High Road

When Jephthah's brothers rejected him, he fled to Tub where a group of scoundrels or worthless men gathered around him. (Judges 11:3). Jephthah was able to unite and mobilize them for God's work. When David was running from Saul, "All those who were in distress or in debt or discontented gathered around David and he became their leader. About four hundred men were with him" (I Samuel 22:2). In spite of their rejection Jephthah and David found others who needed leadership and united them to serve the Lord.

A Picture of the Church.

God does not show favoritism. (Rom. 2:11). God includes all who are willing to put their life on the line for the Lord. Jesus called tax-collectors like Matthew and Zacchaeus. Matthew gave a big reception so Jesus could meet "a great crowd of tax-gatherers." (Luke 5:27-30). Jesus calls sinners. He included the marginalized like the demoniac, the woman at the well and Mary Magdalene from whom he cast out seven devils to join his ministry. No matter where you find yourself, Jesus calls you to join him in being a fisher of men. (Matt. 4:19).

Jesus said when you are invited to a feast, do not take the place of honor. "But take the lowest place, so that when your host comes, he will say to you, 'Friend, move up to a better place' For everyone who exalts himself will be humbled and he who humbles himself will be exalted" (Luke 14:7-11). Are marginalized people welcome in your home and in your church? Being a friend is a million miles from being friendly. It costs little to smile, but it costs more to be a friend.

Jephthah's Foolish Vow

After making two wise moves - recognizing it was the Lord's battle and negotiating rather than taking revenge - Jephthah made a foolish move. He unwisely vowed to God; "If you give the Ammonites into my hands, whatever comes out of the door of my house when I return in triumph will be the Lord's and I will sacrifice it as a burnt offering" (v. 31). When he returned, his daughter, his only child, came out to greet him. In his emotional passion he made a vow in haste that he would regret for ever. He was a man of his word even when keeping his word caused him great pain. His daughter assured him, "My father, you have given your word to the Lord. Do to me just as you promised, now that the Lord has avenged you of your enemies" (Judges 11:36). (Some scholars believe she was not offered as a sacrifice but set apart as a virgin.)

Why was Jephthah included in God's Hall of Fame? Even though his half-brothers drove him away from the family, he chose to talk to the elders of Gilead when they asked him to be their commander and lead them into battle. They recognized his ability as a mighty warrior, assuring Jephthah, they would give him the honor to rule over them. Jephthah led Israel for six years, died and was buried in a town in Gilead.

DAVID

The Man After God's Own Heart

HEBREWS 11:32

The life of David occupies 40 chapters in the Bible. God told the prophet, Samuel, to visit Jesse in Bethlehem because he had chosen one of Jesse's eight sons to be king. (I Sam. 16:1). When Samuel saw Eliab, the first son, he felt sure this was God's choice. The Lord said to Samuel, "Don't think Eliab is the one just because he's tall and handsome. He isn't the one I've chosen. People judge others by what they look like, but I judge people by what is in their hearts" (I Sam. 16:7 CEV). When we judge by outward appearance, we often miss the character qualities that God sees. Ask God to give you eyes to see the heart of others.

A Man After God's Own Heart

God says, "I have found David son of Jesse, a man after my own heart; he will do everything I want him to do" (Acts 13:22). We see David's heart in many of his Psalms. Only when honest emotions and feelings are revealed can we build deep meaningful relationships. "In your presence is fullness of joy, at your right hand there are pleasures for evermore" (Ps. 16:11 AMP). He wrote, "God's goodness and mercy will be with me every day of my life" (Ps. 23:6).

Overcoming Rejection

The three oldest brothers of David were in Saul's army. David's father, Jesse, sent David to inquire concerning their welfare and the status of the battle. When David arrived, the armies of Israel and the Philistines were lined up, facing each other. For forty days Goliath stepped out from the Philistine army defying Israel. When David heard Goliath shouting his usual defiance and saw how Israel's men fled in great fear, he asked, "Who is this uncircumcised Philistine that he should defy the armies of the living God?" Eliab burned with anger when he heard David talking about the flaunts of Goliath and asked, "Why have you come down here... Did you leave those few sheep in the wilderness? I know how conceited you are... You came down only to watch the battle" (I Sam. 17:23-28).

David was able to look past Eliab's anger because he had spent many days and nights cultivating a deep relationship with God as he tended the sheep. The Lord was his shepherd. He knew that even though he walked through the valley of death God's goodness and mercy were with him. (Psalm 23). "Cast your cares on the Lord and he will sustain you; he will never let the righteous fall" (Ps. 55:22).

When David heard the flaunts of Goliath, he told King Saul he would fight Goliath. Saul replied, "You are only a young man, and he has been a warrior from his youth" (I Sam. 17:33). How could a youth like David make this bold presumptuous statement?

No Wasted Experience

David confidently assured King Saul: "I have been taking care of my Father's sheep and goats. When a lion or a bear comes to steal a lamb from the flock, I go after it with a club and rescue the lamb from its mouth. If the animal turns on me, I catch it by the jaws and club it to death. I have done this to both lions and bears, and I'll do it to this pagan Philistine too, for he has defied the armies of the living God." (I Sam. 17:34-36 NLT).

David Defeats the Giant

"The Lord who delivered me from the paw of the lion and the paw of the bear will deliver me from the hand of this Philistine" (I Sam. 17:37). King Saul said, "The Lord be with you." He had David dressed in a coat of armor, bronze helmet and sword. David was not used to the armor and removed them. David took his staff, chose five smooth stones, and with sling in hand he approached the Philistine giant. Goliath cursed David seeing he was only a mere boy and said, "Am I a dog, that you come against me with sticks?... I'll give your flesh to the birds and wild animals." David replied, "This day the Lord will hand you over to me, and I'll strike you down and cut off your head... and the whole world will know that there is a God in Israel. All those gathered here will know that it is not by sword or spear that the Lord saves; for the battle is the Lord's, and he will give all of you into our hands" (17:46-47). As Goliath approached, David ran quickly to meet him taking a stone he slung and struck the giant on the forehead and killed him.

God arranges our lives so that he can use our experiences to mature us for greater ministry. "The steps of a good man (or woman) are ordered by the Lord" (Ps. 37:23 KJV).

We all face difficult situations. Our "lions and bears" may be a desperate work situation, a dysfunctional family, a community with violence, poor schools, corrupt leaders, chronic physical pain, divorce or an unhealthy church situation. Allow God to train you and develop your character for greater ministry. Petition God to remove your situation. If the door opens, walk through the door. However, God may be saying you need to stay and be the salt and light. Give yourself wholeheartedly to him. Claim his grace to be all that God wants you to be in your undesirable situation.

Compassion and Comfort Can Be By-products of Your Trials

It's your choice—seek God and obey him or struggle on your own. Paul wrote, "Praise... be to the God of all comfort, who comforts us in all our troubles, so that we can comfort those in any trouble with the comfort we ourselves have received from God. For just as the suffering of Christ flows over into our lives, so also through Christ, our comfort overflows" (II Cor. 1:3-5). If you experience a divorce, you can comfort others in this situation. If you are learning to overcome your anger, you are better equipped to help others with anger issues. If you have a strong-willed child, you can encourage and comfort other parents who have a strong-willed child. We are able to help others by leading them to the source of comfort we have received through Jesus. It's a choice we make, to seek God or continue to struggle. Don't waste your experiences.

Overcome Sin

From his balcony, King David saw Bathsheba bathing. He sent for her and committed adultery resulting in her pregnancy. He tried to cover his sin by calling Bathsheba's husband, Uriah, home from the army and encouraged Uriah to go home and be with his wife. Uriah was a loyal soldier. He said, "The ark and Israel and Judah are staying in tents... How could I go to my house?" David commanded Joab, his army general, to place Uriah in the front lines where he was killed.

Sin Brings Consequences

David did not deal decisively with the sins of his family. His family feuds escalated into murder and treason. His son, Ammon raped his sister, Tamar. This enraged Tamar's brother, Absalom, who then killed his half-brother Ammon. (II Sa. 13:1). Absalom went into hiding for three years which broke David's heart because he loved Absalom. Later, Absalom plotted against David to take away his throne. David had to learn the hard way. "The way of the transgressor is hard." (Proverb 13:15 KJV). "Be sure your sin will find you out" (Num. 32:23). Whatever we sow we will reap. (Gal. 6:7).

Today, many parents like David are fearful of disciplining their children—feeling their children will not like them. David's son, Absalom, turned against his parents. Jesus said, "Parents will betray their own children and children will turn against their parents and have them killed" (Matt. 10:21 TEV). Absalom died in disgrace all alone.

David was forbidden to build the temple because he was a man of war. (I Chronicles 28:3). Sin can be forgiven, but we live with the painful consequences. Today, many families are torn apart. Sin brings death, death to your dreams and hopes. Men and women marry for the wrong reason, resulting in pain. Many are caught in the trap of pornography resulting in poor or broken marriages. Others "enjoy" drugs which often lead to suicide.

David's Response to Sin

How could David be in God's Hall of Fame? Notice how David responds when he sins. God was angry with David when he took a census of all the fighting men in Judah and Israel. "David was conscious-stricken after he had counted the fighting men, and he said to the Lord, 'O Lord, I beg you, take away the guilt of your servant. I have done a very foolish thing.'" He made a clear confession. God's punishment was great: seventy thousand people in Israel died. (II Samuel 24:10, 15). God permitted Satan to tempt David, revealing his pride. Why would the nation have to suffer when it was David who sinned? (II Sam. 24:17). Maybe because it was not only David's sin but also the sin of the people who wanted to know how strong their military was, indicating they placed their trust in man rather than God. God was grieved because of the suffering of his people and called off further punishment, revealing his mercy. (II Sam. 24:16).

David Expresses His Sorrow

Not only did David beg God for forgiveness, but also he asked God to punish him and his family and spare the people. He expressed his sorrow: "Have mercy on me, O God, according to your unfailing love; according to your great compassion, blot out my transgression. Wash away all my iniquity and cleanse me from my sin. For I know my transgressions, and my sin is always before me. Against you, you only, have I sinned and done what is evil in your sight, so that you are proved right when you speak and justified when you judge" (Ps. 51:1-4).

Forgiveness Brings Joy

"Oh, what joy for those whose rebellion is forgiven, whose sin is put out of sight! Yes, what joy for those whose record the Lord has cleared of sin, whose lives are lived in complete honesty! When I refused to confess my sin, I was weak and miserable, and I groaned all day long... Finally, I confessed all my sins to you and stopped trying to hide them. I said to myself, 'I will confess my rebellion to the Lord.' And you forgave me! All my guilt is gone" (Ps. 32:1-5 NLT).

There are times when we confess our sins to God but still don't feel forgiven. In this situation it will help you to let another person be your priest as James 5:16 says, "Confess your sins to each other and pray for each other so you may be healed."

David Strengthens Himself in the Lord

When David's army discovered the Amalekites had burned the city of Ziklag and carried away their wives and children, his soldiers were ready to stone David. What did David do in this desperate situation? He strengthened himself in the Lord. (I Sam. 30:6). He asked God what to do and followed his guidance. He and his army rescued their wives and children. They recovered everything the Amalekites had taken. (I Sam. 30:18). Have you learned to throw yourself on God's mercy and strengthen yourself in the Lord? "Come near to God and he will come near to you" (James 4:8).

David Betrayed

David writes about his betrayal: "If an enemy were insulting me, I could endure it; if a foe were rising against me, I could hide. But it is you, a man like myself, my companion, my close friend, with whom I once enjoyed sweet fellowship at the house of God, as we walked about among the worshipers. Let death take my enemies by surprise; let them go down alive to the realm of the dead, for evil finds lodging among them" (Ps. 55:12-15).

David wanted justice and revenge. He called to God in distress morning, noon and night. He knew that God heard him. (Ps. 55:16-17). Is your heart broken when you commit sin? Too often we are flippant and take a casual attitude concerning our sin. We think, "Jesus died for my sin so I am fine." Insincerity is repulsive to God. Don't presume on God's love and grace. "A broken and contrite heart, Oh God, you will not despise" (Ps. 51:17). If there is no repentance, there is no forgiveness. Don't presume on God's love and grace. Don't try to bury your pain by denying it. Ask God for his grace and ask a trusted friend to pray and walk with you to find forgiveness and healing. David writes, (v. 18), "He rescues me unharmed from the battle waged against me, even though many oppose me." David was able to rise above the backstabbing. Like David, I too become stronger through times of testing.

David Won the Hearts of the People

Many times, David risked his life for his people. He won their hearts by serving them by laying down his life for them. Jesus said, "Greater love has no one than this, that he lay down his life for his friends. You are my friends if you do what I command" (John 15:13-14). His motivation was not for himself but so others would find life. For whom are you laying down your life?

David's Respect for God's Anointed

David's loyalty to King Saul was amazing. King Saul was jealous of David because the hearts of the people were for David. Saul spent years trying to kill David, even sending his army to find him. On several occasions David refused to kill King Saul or to allow any of his men to kill him because he was God's anointed. (I Samuel 18-24). David showed kindness to Mephibosheth, son of Jonathan and grandson of King Saul, when there was nothing politically to be gained from that act. (II Sam. 21:7-9). David based his actions on what he knew God wanted him to do, not on what would increase his power. With each demonstration of character, his influence increased.

David was included in God's Hall of Fame and recognized by God as a man after God's own heart. Because when he sinned, he was truly repentant, a quality so often lacking in today's Christians. David followed through with full determination to serve the Lord no matter what the cost. He expresses his desire: "One thing have I asked of the Lord, that will I seek after, inquire for and [insistently] require, that I may dwell in the house of the Lord - in His presence... to meditate, consider and inquire in His temple" (Psalm 27:4 AMP). Make that the desire of your heart and you too will be in God's Hall of Fame.

SAMUEL

Ask of the Lord

HEBREWS 11:32

"The Lord was with Samuel as he grew up, and he let none of Samuel's words fall to the ground. And all Israel from Dan to Beersheba recognized that Samuel was attested as a prophet of the Lord" (I Sa. 3:19-20).

Samuel is unique in that we have a window into his childhood and youth. Samuel was born to Elkanah and Hannah, faithful followers of God. Elkanah had two wives, Hannah and Peninnah. (I Sam. 1:2). Peninnah had children, but Hannah was barren. Year after year, when the family went to the temple of the Lord, Peninnah would taunt Hannah because she was barren. Hannah, in deep anguish and grief, cried out to God for a child. She vowed that, if God would grant her a child, she would dedicate him to the Lord. (I Sam. 1:10-16). Eli, the priest, saw Hannah praying in anguish and thought she was drunk. She assured him she was pouring out her soul to the Lord. Eli answered, "Go in peace, and may the God of Israel grant you what you have asked of him" (I Sam. 1:17). Hannah gave birth and named the child, Samuel, meaning, "asked of God." Hannah kept her promise. As soon as Samuel was weaned, she took him to the temple to be a servant to Eli. She said, "I gave him to the Lord. For his whole life he will be given over to the Lord" (I Sam. 1:28).

Pass on Your Faith

One of the weaknesses of our American culture is our image of a homemaker. Motherhood and homemaking are not second-rate careers. Many girls are more concerned about a career and only give second thought to raising a family. As a teenager my wife, Helen, helped to care for nieces and nephews and others. This experience was excellent training for raising our family.

Hannah prayed for her child before he was conceived. As parents, it is important that you pray for your child before conception. Many married couples are unable to have children. Ask God to bless your marriage union with children. If, for some reason, that does not come to fulfillment, pray for God's grace to accept your situation and to incline your heart to serve him. You may want to adopt a child or be a foster parent. This will be your primary mission while your children are being raised.

Samuel was dedicated to the Lord before he was born. God chose Jeremiah to speak to the nations before he was born. Before your children are born pray for them, sing to them in the womb and in their infancy. Dedicate them to the Lord in a public ceremony. Share God's love and the salvation story. As you share the many stories of the Bible, they will catch your enthusiasm and love for God and his word. (Luke 18:15-17). While the church is very important, don't depend on the church to do all the training. The home and the church need to support each other.

Trian Your Children to Hear God's Voice

As Samuel lived with Eli in the temple, God called his name, waking him from sleep. Samuel went to Eli and asked him what he wanted. This happened three times until Eli realized it was God calling. Eli told Samuel to answer, "Speak, Lord your servant is listening" (I Sam. 3:9).

Train your children to hear God's voice. Share how God speaks to you. Jesus said, "My sheep hear my voice." This is not some mystical exercise. Pray, read his word, let God direct your thoughts and steps. Learn to be conscious of God's presence. Walking with Jesus is fulfilling and exciting.

God's Message May Be Disturbing

God gave Samuel a disturbing message. His message was that God is going to punish Eli for not disciplining his sons. Eli knew God's instruction. (Deut. 6). Eli was responsible to teach his sons to love God with all their heart, soul and strength. He was to impress these commands on his children when they got up in the morning, throughout the day, when they ate and when they went to bed. Moses wrote, "Tie these commandments as symbols on your hands and on your forehead. Write them on the doorframes of your house and on your gates." (Deut. 6:7-9).

Unfortunately, Samuel, like Eli, was unable to bring his sons into a close relationship with God. "The nation's leaders came to Samuel and said, 'You are an old man. You set a good example for your sons, but they haven't followed it. Now we want a king to be our leader, just like all the other nations. Choose one for us!'" (I Sam. 8:4-5).

Was Samuel so occupied on being God's judge and prophet that he neglected his own children? Our primary ministry is always to our own family. Church leaders were clearly instructed, "Manage your family well and see that your children obey the Lord with proper respect. If anyone does not know how to manage his own family, how can he take care of God's church?" (I Tim. 3:4-5). "May the words of my mouth and the meditations of my heart be pleasing in your sight, O Lord, my Rock and my Redeemer" (Ps. 19:14). Like Eli, we are often blind to our sins. "The sins of some are obvious, reaching the place of judgment ahead of them; the sins of others trail behind them" (I Tim. 5:24).

Are you spending quality time with your family? Today, many parents are absorbed with earning a living and have little time for face-to-face interaction with each other or their children. Without quality time, your children will lose respect for you. Pray with your children before you put them to bed. Eat together as a family. Take time to memorize a bible verse and talk about how the verse relates to their life? There are no perfect parents, so when you fall short, ask Jesus to forgive you as well as your spouse and children.

I was exceedingly blessed to have parents who read their Bible and prayed. They instilled in me the necessity to exercise these disciplines daily. Mother would play hymns on the piano, and we sang together. A motto that made a deep impression on me hung in my bedroom. It read: "Your life will soon be past, only what is done for Christ will last." Another plaque read, "Say nothing you would not want to be saying when Jesus comes. Do nothing you would not want to be doing when Jesus comes. Go nowhere you would not want to be when Jesus comes."

Samuel—A Man of Prayer

"As for me, far be it from me that I should sin against the Lord by failing to pray for you. I will teach you the way that is good and right. But be sure to fear the Lord and serve him faithfully with all your heart; consider what great things he has done for you. Yet, if you persist in doing evil, both you and your king will be swept away." (I Sam. 12:23-25).

Do You Pray for Our Nation?

"I urge, first of all, that request, prayers of intercession and thanksgiving be made for everyone—for kings and all those in authority, that we may live peaceful and quiet lives in all godliness and holiness. This is good, and pleases God our Savior, who wants all men to be saved and to come to a knowledge of the truth. For there is one God and one mediator between God and men, the man Christ Jesus." (I Timothy 2:1-5). Many Christians have conformed to the world. "Do not be conformed any longer to the patterns of this world but be transformed by the renewing of your mind. Then you will be able to test and approve what God's will is - his good, pleasing and perfect will." (Romans 12:1-2). "Do not love the world or anything in the world. If anyone loves the world, the love of the Father is not in him. For everything in the world - the craving of sinful man, the lust of his eyes and the boasting of what he has and does—comes not from the Father but from the world. The world and its desires pass away, but the man who does the will of God lives forever." (I John 2:15-17).

Israel Wanted a King Like Other Nations

Samuel was the last and most effective of the judges. He also became a prophet to the nations. God had Samuel warn the nation that asking for a king to be their ruler was not good, because they would look to their king rather than to Jehovah God to deliver them.

The people deliberately chose to go against God's design. "The Lord told Samuel, 'Do what they want. Give them a king'" (I Sam. 8:22 CEV). Because of the hardness of their hearts, God instructed Samuel to anoint King David and later King Solomon. God will often give us what we desire even if it is wrong. "God gave them what they asked for but sent a wasting disease upon them" (Ps. 106:15). "God gave them over to their stubborn hearts to follow their own devices" (Ps. 81:12). Be sure your desires line up with God's will.

Like Israel, who insisted on having a king like those around us, we too often want to be like others around us. Too often there is little difference between people of the world and people of the church. Money and materialism drive us so we don't have time for God. Our kingdom is more important than God's Kingdom. (Matt. 6:33). Do we really know what Jesus meant when he said we are to deny ourselves and take up our cross and follow him? (Luke 9:23).

Let Others Help You

The pressures are so great to conform to the patterns of this world, that we need to be in a small group of disciples who hold each other accountable. The early church met in small groups. They turned the world upside down. (Acts 17:6). We have adopted the world's philosophy, "It's none of your business what I do." We don't need each other. This philosophy has infiltrated the church so that we don't think it is our responsibility to care enough to confront one another. This results in an anemic church. We can pray for revival but there is nothing to revive because too often we have lost our first love. We have lost our zeal and enthusiasm.

God gives us a clear formula for getting us out of our weakened state. God says: "If my people, who are called by name, will humble themselves and pray and seek my face and turn from their wicked ways, then will I hear from heaven and will forgive their sin and will heal their land. Now my eyes will be open and my ears attentive to the prayers offered in this place." (II Chronicles 7:14). The key is repentance. There is no reviving, no grace without repentance.

"AND THE PROPHETS"

HEBREWS 11:32

The Old Testament in the Bible consists of 39 books. The five books of the Law, Genesis to Deuteronomy, are also known as the Torah. The books of history are Joshua through Esther. The books of wisdom sometimes referred to as Books of Poetry are Job through the Song of Solomon. These books are followed by the concluding seventeen books of the Old Testament known as "The Prophets" Isaiah through Malachi.

In the first thirty-two verses of Hebrews 11, God's Hall of Faith Chapter, Paul lists seventeen men and women of faith, Abel through Samuel. Verse 32: "What more shall I say? I do not have time to tell about Gideon, Barak, Samson and Jephthah, about David and Samuel and the prophets."

"And the Prophets"

The concluding chapters of this book focus on the final phrase of v. 32, "and the prophets." These seventeen books cover approximately three hundred forty years between 740-400 BC. These seventeen books, occupying nearly one fourth of the bible, are often ignored. We shy away from the prophets because their message is permeated with judgment. No one wants to be told the consequences of their sin. The common theme of the prophets is the abuse of religion. However, it is very reassuring that all the prophets present a sure hope in the coming of the Messiah even though, like us, they were living in a fallen and perverse world.

Don't Neglect these Books

Can we say we take the bible seriously when we neglect the books of prophesy? Peter says, "I have written both letters, (I and II Peter), as reminders to stimulate you to wholesome thinking. I want you to recall the words spoken in the past by the holy prophets, and the command given by our Lord and Savior." (II Peter 3:1-2). Apparently, Peter had to remind the early church not to neglect the message of the prophetic books.

Difficult Assignment

It wasn't easy being a prophet. "The Lord warned Israel and Judah by all the prophets and the seers, saying, 'Turn from your evil ways, and keep My commandments and My statutes, according to all the law which I commanded your fathers and which I sent to you by my servants the prophets'" (II Kings. 17:13 AMP). "The Lord sent word through his messengers again and again... But they mocked God's messengers, despised his words and scoffed at his prophets until the wrath of the Lord was aroused against his people and there was no remedy" (II Chron. 36:15-16).

The prophets preached repentance, judgment, impending destruction, sin, and in general how displeased God was over the behavior of his people. Prophets were not the most popular people in town (unless they were false prophets and said just what the people wanted to hear). The biblical prophets were not concerned about being popular. Their concern was obedience to God and faithfully proclaiming his word.

The prophets had a double focus. First, their message was given to build and encourage the few faithful believers to remain steadfast for God. Second, they warned the wicked nations of God's judgment, while powerfully calling on them to repent and turn from their sins.

"The Biblical prophets continue to be the most powerful and effective voices of this earth for keeping religion honest, humble, and compassionate. The prophets sniff out injustice, especially injustice that was dressed up in religious garb... and especially hypocrisy that assumes a religious pose. None of us can be trusted... We must keep company with these Biblical prophets. We are required to submit all our words and acts to their passionate scrutiny to prevent the perversion of our religion into something self-serving. A spiritual life that doesn't give a large place to the prophets will end up making us worse instead of better and separating us from God's ways instead of drawing us into them."[23]

Miracles of God

Paul enumerated some of the great miracles of God which occurred through the years of the prophets' ministry. "I do not have time to tell you... of the prophets who, through faith, conquered kingdoms, administered justice, and gained what was promised; who shut the mouths of lions, quenched the fury of the flames, and escaped the edge of the sword; whose weakness was turned to strength; and who became powerful in battle and routed foreign armies. Women received back their dead, raised to life again" (Heb. 11:32-35).

Important Transition

Americans must not overlook the following. "Others were tortured to death with clubs, refusing to accept release, [offered in terms of denying their faith], that they might be resurrected to a better life. Others had to suffer the trial of mocking and scourging and even chains and imprisonment. They were stoned to death... sawn asunder; they were slaughtered by the sword; they had to go about wrapped in the skins of sheep and goats, utterly destitute, oppressed, cruelly treated, [Men] of whom the world was not worthy, roaming over the desolate places and the mountains, and [living] in caves and caverns and holes of the earth. And all of these, thought they won divine approval by [means of] their faith, did not receive the fulfillment of what was promised, because God had us in mind and had something better and greater in view for us, so that they [these heroes and heroines of faith] should not come to perfection apart from us, [that is, before we could join them]" (Heb. 11:35-40 AMP).

---

23 Introduction to Amos in NIV/The Message Parallel Study Bible. Zondervan 2008

We Suffer for Neglecting One-Fourth of the Bible

By ignoring God's message given through the prophets, we have an anemic or feeble perception of God. Without a respectful fear of God, we lose our passion. "The fear of the Lord is the beginning of wisdom and knowledge of the Holy One is understanding" (Prov. 9:10). When we lose reverent fear, we lose the Holy Spirit's fire and our culture loses its way. The message of the prophets will move us from being lukewarm to becoming zealous for God. Today, as in their day, we often have a form of godliness but the power is lacking, since there is little respect for God. (II Tim. 3:5). We read the Scriptures, but do selective reading. We gloss over those passages that speak of God's discipline and judgment.

Window into World Events

The prophets are a window into why we have so much suffering and evil today. They spoke openly concerning sin and the sins of the nations. "When disaster comes to a city, has not the Lord caused it? Surely the Sovereign Lord does nothing without revealing his plan to His servants the prophets" (Amos 3:6-7 AMP). We bring the suffering on ourselves by our indifference to God's message.

God has always warned the world of coming judgments, in order that God may not need to bring the judgement. He warned Noah of the coming flood, Abraham and Lot of the future destruction of Sodom, told Joseph of the seven years' famine, Moses of the ten plagues on Egypt and Jonah of the destruction of Nineveh. Various prophets were told in detail of the final events in connection with the captivities of God-chosen people. In every case, the warnings were shockingly executed. In the case of Nineveh, the judgment was postponed after Jonah's preaching, but when later generations of Ninevites backslid, the warning of Nahum was carried out completely against them. Christ's coming was foretold from Genesis to Malachi.

God is in control of all world events. The foundations are shaking. Often, he is the one who is doing the shaking to awaken us from our lethargy. God is omniscient (all-knowing), omnipotent (all powerful) and omnipresence (everywhere present). He directs the nations as well as directing our individual lives. This gives us a holy boldness that carries over in our daily lives, enabling us to be pillars of strength to those around us. The prophet's message will light a fire in our hearts so we, like the apostles, cannot keep quiet about what we experience. (Acts 4:20).

"Where there is no revelation, (no message from the prophets) the people cast off restraint." (Proverbs 29:18). The inevitable result is that we, like Israel, give our allegiance to other "gods."

Our Downward Spiral

Who have you met lately that is hungry to know God? Who is on fire with enthusiasm for Jesus? I'm not talking about emotionalism, I'm talking about a holy boldness. The vast majority of people have very little consciousness that we will all one day stand before a holy God who demands perfection. Only a very few have a passion to share the Good News with their peers, neighbors or even their relatives. The Great Commission is not the great suggestions of Jesus. Jesus' commission is for everyone to make disciples at home and to the ends of the earth. (Matt. 28:19-20). These final words are not the driving force of our life as Jesus intended them to be. How many disciple makers do you know? Jesus said, "I tell you this, that you must give an account on judgment day of every idle word you speak. The words you say now reflect your fate then, either you will be justified by them or you will be condemned" (Matt. 12:36-37 NLT).

Christians tend to justify "little things" that hinder our walk with Jesus. These "little things" rob us of the confidence and the power of the Holy Spirit. These "little things" put out the Holy Spirit's fire" (I Thess. 5:19). Have we ever had the "Holy Spirit's fire?" Jeremiah said, "His word is in my heart like a fire, a fire shut up in my bones. I am weary of holding it in; indeed, I cannot" (Jer. 20:9). We set aside our bible and prayer time because we have more "important" things to do. Our schedules are full of worldly pursuits.

Why Suffering and Evil, Jesus and the Prophets

Jesus left no question as to the importance of the prophets. Jesus said, in the parable of the Rich Man and Lazarus, that the Rich

Man died and went to hell, (Hades), where he suffered torment. He looked up and saw Abraham and Lazarus. He begged Abraham to send Lazarus to his father's house to warm them not to come to this place of torment. Abraham replied, "They have Moses and the Prophets; let them listen to them." 'No, father Abraham,' he said, 'but if someone from the dead goes to them, they will repent.' "He said to him, 'If they do not listen to Moses and the Prophets, they will not be convinced even if someone rises from the dead'" (Luke 16:30-31).

The Coming of the Messiah

The prophets spoke clearly concerning the coming of the Messiah. Jesus referring to the Old Testament, especially the prophets, said to the Jews, "You diligently study the Scriptures because you think that by them you possess eternal life. These are the Scriptures that testify about me, yet you refuse to come to me to have life" (John 5:39-40). On the road to Emmaus, Jesus said to the disciples: "How foolish you are, and how slow of heart to believe all that the prophets have spoken! Did not Christ have to suffer these things and then enter his glory?" (Luke 24:25-26). The book of Matthew refers to the Old Testament prophets thirteen times.

Peter proclaims: "Jesus must remain in heaven until the time comes for God to restore everything, as he promised long ago though the holy prophets" (Acts 2:21). Luke quotes the prophet Zechariah, "God has raised up a horn of salvation for us... as he said through his holy prophets of long ago" (Luke 1:69-70 and Jer. 23:5). The angel in Revelation 10:7 says, "The mystery of God will be accomplished, just as he announced to his servants the prophets."

Paul, in speaking primarily of the Old Testament, writes: "All Scripture is God-breathed and is useful for teaching, rebuking, correcting and training in righteousness, so that the man of God may be thoroughly equipped for every good work" (II Tim. 3:16-17). "Everything that was written in the past was written to teach us, so that through endurance and the encouragement of the Scriptures we might have hope" (Romans 15:4). In referring to Israel's and God's punishment, Paul writes: "Now these things occurred as examples to keep us from setting our hearts on evil things as they did" (I Cor. 10:6). In v. 11 he repeats: "These things happened to them as examples and were written down as warnings for us, on whom the fulfillment of the ages has come."

Forthtelling and Foretelling

Perhaps the forthtelling, that is, God's word for our daily living, is even more important than the foretelling. Foretelling is more dramatic so we often focus on foretelling and push the forthtelling in the background. The prophets spoke clearly against the sins of their day. However, all the prophets promised God's blessings on the people if they were willing to repent and recognize God as sovereign. We need the forthtelling (the warnings) of the prophets to remind us that we must be holy as God is holy in all we do, or we cannot see the Lord. (I Peter 1:15-16 and Hebrews 12:14).

As Christians, we know that our righteousness is not in striving to keep the law but only in the blood of Jesus that atones for our sin. Nevertheless, we are to "work out our salvation with fear and trembling." To do that, we need clear instruction and warning given by these prophets, so we don't wander off from God's design for our lives.

Compare Old Testament with New Testament Prophets

After Pentecost, the role of the prophets changed from a recognized office to individuals who exercise the gift of giving a message from the Lord. New Testament prophets are different from preachers. Prophet and prophecy were used of ordinary Christians who spoke not with absolute divine authority as Old Testament prophets, but simply reported something God had laid on their hearts or brought to their minds. It's clear that the New Testament prophets did not have the authority of the Old Testaments prophets. The New Testament prophets were to be tested by the congregation. It seems they had less authority than that of recognized Bible teaching in the early church.

I have had prophets in the churches I pastored, but I did not give them a public title as I did for pastors, elders or evangelists. Prophets are persons whom the Spirit empowers to speak a word from the Lord. At Pentecost, Peter clearly stated: "In the last days,

God says, I will pour out my Spirit on all people. Your sons and daughters will prophesy, your young men will see visions, your old men will dream dreams. Even on my servants, both men and women, I will pour out my Spirit in those days, and they will prophesy" (Acts 2:17-18).

In speaking of Jesus giving the church gifts, Paul writes: "It was Christ who gave some to be apostles, some to be prophets, some to be evangelists and some to be pastors and teachers, to prepare God's people for works of service, so that the body of Christ may be build up until we all reach unity in the faith and in the knowledge of the Son of God and become mature, attaining to the whole measure of the fullness of Christ" (Eph. 4:11-23). Are you aware of churches who have individuals who are called to function in the office of apostle? There are a few churches who emphasize the five-fold ministry as Paul sets forth in Ephesians 4. I believe Paul meant for this list of gifts to be suggestive rather than definitive. There are thirty or more gifts listed in Corinthians and Romans and throughout the Scriptures. Many churches today have youth ministers, worship leaders, ministers of music, and many other positions which may also suggest that these five offices are not definitive.

Paul wrote Ephesians 4:11-13 passage in AD 60. About ten years prior to writing Ephesians he refers to prophets as he writes to the Thessalonians: "Do not spurn the gifts and utterances of the prophets—do not depreciate prophetic revelations nor despise inspired instruction or exhortation or warning. But test and prove all things [until you can recognize] what is good; [to that] hold fast" (I Thess. 5:20-21 Amp). Other passages referring to the prophets as Romans 12, I Corinthians 12-14 were all written before Ephesians 4:11-13. But note the contrast with the books following the writing of Ephesians. He makes very little reference to the prophetic gift in any of these letters. He wrote Philippians in AD 61 in which he makes no mention of prophets, but rather addresses the elders/overseers and deacons. Four to six years after Paul wrote Ephesians, he wrote first and second Timothy instructing Timothy to appoint elders and deacons. He did not mention prophets. This chronology indicates to me that the office of apostles was largely replaced by elders and deacons.

Prophets Today

Prophecy provides opportunity for everyone to participate in the worship, not just those who are skilled communicators or who have gifts of teaching. Paul affirms Peter by writing that he wants all the Corinthians to prophesy (I Cor. 14:5). And he says, "For you can all prophesy in turn (one by one), so that everyone may be instructed and encouraged" (v. 31). Paul makes it clear that prophets are in control of what they say. "Two or three prophets should speak, and the others should weigh carefully what is said. And if a revelation comes to someone who is sitting down, the first speaker should stop. For you can all prophesy in turn so that everyone may be instructed and encouraged. The spirit of prophets is subject to the control of prophets. For God is not a God of disorder but of peace—as in all the congregations of the Lord's people" (I Cor. 14:29-32). In the New Testament, the testing of a prophet's message needs to be evaluated immediately by the other prophets as well as all who are present. (I Thess. 5:20-21).

Our present church structure makes it difficult to integrate prophecy into the life of the church. This gift would be utilized more frequently and effectively in small groups where we are free to encourage and admonish one another.

How do we spot those with the gift of prophecy? Prophets have an inner compulsion to speak the truth about sin, especially sins of hypocrisy, dishonesty or taking advantage of others. Peter confronted Ananias and Sapphira in a forceful manner (Acts 5:1-11). John the Baptist forcefully calls for repentance. (Luke 3:1-20). Prophets are direct and often blunt and therefore may be misunderstood. They expect immediate outward change. They support their words with Biblical examples.

I have chosen several of these seventeen prophets who wrote the books of prophecy, Isaiah through Malachi, to help and challenge us to understand more of God's greatness and, most of all, his love and passion for his people. These Old Testament prophets who warned of God's judgment also spoke of the restored peace and prosperity that will follow God's judgment. They held forth a clear message of hope and peace for those who were obedient to God's message.

ISAIAH

Holiness

Isaiah is the king of the prophets. His name means "the Lord is salvation." His command of the Hebrew language indicated he was highly educated. He had royal blood which helped to open the door for him to talk with the kings of Judah and Israel: Uzziah, Jotham, Ahaz and Hezekiah. His uncle was King Amaziah of Judah. His ministry covered approximately sixty years during the last half of the eighth century B.C. Tradition says his death came as he was sawn in two by wicked King Manasseh, the son of King Hezekiah. (Hebrews 11:37).

Isaiah's Calling

Isaiah's call to be God's prophet came when he had a vision of God. (Isaiah 6). He saw the angels around the throne of God calling: "Holy, holy, holy is the Lord almighty; the whole earth is full of his glory" (6:3). "Woe is me!" I cried, "I am ruined, for I am a man of unclean lips, and I live among a people of unclean lips, and my eyes have seen the King, the Lord Almighty" (v. 5). Only after God touched him, was he qualified to be sent as God's messenger of warning. (Is. 6:8). Like Isaiah, God cannot use us until we recognize his holiness and confess and repent of our sinfulness.

Words of Warning

Prophecies concerning the Day of the Lord foretell a time of awesome and frightening events leading to the return of Christ. Men will hide in caves (Isaiah 2:19-21), the earth will be shaken (13:13), and will become almost vacant and a total waste. It's war time. (24:1, 3, 6; 31:8-9). Babylon will be destroyed (47:1-9). The time of God's wrath will come to an end when "the great trumpet will be blown" (27:13). (Rev. 11:5).

Chapters one through 39 speak of the judgment. "I reared children...but they have rebelled against me. The ox knows its master, the donkey his owner's manger but Israel does not know... or understand." (1:2-3). Chapters 13-39 describe judgment of all nations. However, Isaiah 40-66 are some of the most encouraging chapters in the bible. These chapters are saturated with messages of hope referring to Christ and his coming kingdom.

Prophecies Concerning Christ

Isaiah provides us with more information concerning the coming of Christ than any other Old Testament prophet. (2:4; 4:2; 7:14; 8:8-14; 9:6-9; 11:1-2, etc.). His final chapters portray deliverance and mercy for God's people. (Is. 61:3-14). Everything is leading up to the peaceful eternal government of God and finally, to the "new heaven and a new earth" (Is. 65:17).

The Holy One of Israel

"Isaiah refers to God as the 'Holy One of Israel' 26 times. In all, the other prophetic books combine this phrase only six times."[24] Isaiah portrays God as holy and employs the term "holy" 58 times in his 66 chapters which is more than any other biblical author except Moses' book of Leviticus. Holiness is a primary doctrine throughout the Bible, appearing nearly six hundred times.

What Does It Mean to Be Holy?

"God chose us in Christ before the foundation of the world; that we should be holy (consecrated and set apart for Him)" (Eph.1:4 AMP). "Do not conform to the evil desires you had... for it is written: 'Be holy, because I am holy.'" (Lev. 11:14; I Peter 1:14-16). We cannot make ourselves holy, it is Christ who makes us holy. "We are made holy because Christ obeyed God and offered himself

---

24 NIV Study Bible, Introduction to Isaiah.

once for all" (Heb. 10:10 CEV). We are not holy unless we are wholly his.

The Foundation of Holiness

"To say that God is holy means that he is completely separate from all evil or defect. God is completely and perfectly good. The Lord is worthy of total allegiance, exclusive worship, and loving obedience. We are called to be holy because God is holy. (Lev. 11:44-45; 19:2; 20:7; 21:8). A business act is ethical if it reflects God's holy-just-loving character. We reflect God's holiness when we... behave with purity, accountability, and humility. Holiness is not only about individuals' behavior..., but about how what each person does affects the whole people of God. To be holy is to go beyond the law to love your neighbor, to love even your enemy, and to 'be perfect, therefore, as your heavenly Father is perfect' (Matt. 5:48, echoing Lev. 19:2)."[25]

"You are God's people, so don't let it be said that any of you are immoral or indecent or greedy. Don't use dirty or foolish or filthy words. Instead, say how thankful you are. Being greedy, indecent, or immoral is just another way of worshipping idols. You can be sure that people who behave in this way will never be part of the kingdom that belongs to Christ and to God" (Eph. 5:3-5 CEV).

"We are not destined to happiness, nor to health, but to holiness. Today we have far too many desires and interests, and our lives are being consumed and wasted by them. Many of them may be right and good... God must cause their importance to us to decrease. The thing that truly matters is whether a person will accept the God who will make him holy. God has only one intended destiny for mankind—holiness. His only goal is to produce saints. God is not some eternal blessing-machine for people to use. He did not come to save us out of pity—He came to save us because He created us to be holy..."[26]

Our highest calling is to be holy, i.e. set apart from sin. If you have known sin in your life, you are blocking God's power, making

---

25 This section is adapted from The Bible Commentary/Produced by TOW Project, The Foundational Concept of Holiness in Leviticus.

26 Oswald Chambers in *My Upmost for His Highest,* devotional for September 1.

you unholy and ineffective. Your joy is gone, resulting in a lukewarm and frustrating life. Sincerely repent and claim Christ's atonement, his sacrificial gift of himself and receive Christ's gift of holiness. When we are wholly his, we open the door to abundant living. The supernatural becomes natural.

Being Holy Does Not Mean an Easy Life

Does that mean we will have an easy life? Certainly not. Isaiah and all the prophets were criticized continually. They suffered and often needed to stand alone. But Isaiah reminds us, God "gives us strength... and increases the power of the weak. Even youths grow tired and weary, and young men stumble and fall; but those who hope in the Lord will renew their strength. They will soar on wings like eagles; they will run and not grow weary, they will walk and not be faint" (Is. 40:29-31).

God Cannot Tolerate Sin

Many believe they have done good deeds which they think qualifies them to meet God. Isaiah promises his rebellious people redemption if they repent and commit themselves to obey God. He depicts God's justice in clear and direct terms. The judgment that will be unleashed upon all the nations that deny God is called "the Day of the Lord." Isaiah employees such terms as "anger" 26x, wrath 8x, fire 39x, and punish 5x which give us a window to a God of justice. God's wrath is his righteous reaction to our sin. God is in complete control of his emotions. David reminds us that "God is a righteous judge, a God who displays his wrath every day" (Ps. 7:11). "You hate all who do wrong" (Ps. 5:5). "The wicked and those who love violence his soul hates" (Ps. 11:5). However, "God will have compassion on his people. He will rescue them like he rescued Israel when they crossed the Red Sea. (43:2, 16-19). God hated sin so much that he gave his only Son so we can be forgiven of our sin. (John 3:16). He will bring peace and safety as he reigns in justice and righteousness. All nations will stream to Jerusalem, "the City of the Lord." (Is. 60:14).

Isaiah paints a picture of Jesus ruling God's kingdom on earth. "This is the goal toward which the book of Isaiah steadily moves. The restored earth and the restored people will then conform to the divine ideal, and all will result in the praise and glory of the Holy One of Israel for what he has accomplished."[27]

Our Compassionate and Great God

Isaiah chapter 40 depicts God's greatness: "All men are like grass, and all their glory is like the flowers of the field... The grass withers and the flowers fall, but the word of our God stands forever... the Sovereign Lord comes with power... He tends his flock like a shepherd: He gathers the lambs in his arms and carries them close to his heart; he gently leads those that have young...

"Who has measured the waters in the hallow of his hand?... Who has weighed the mountains on the scales?... The nations are like a drop in a bucket; regarded as dust on the scales; ... Before him, the nations are as nothing; they are regarded by him as worthless and less than nothing... He sits enthroned above the circle of the earth, and its people are like grasshoppers... He brings princes to naught and reduces the rulers of this world to nothing... He blows over them and they wither, and a whirlwind sweeps them away like chaff.... Lift your eyes and look to the heavens; He brings out the starry host one by one, and calls them each by name..." (Isaiah 40).

Even though Isaiah is portraying the justice of God, his message will lift you to new heights, so you can soar with the eagles and let the supernatural become natural even in the darkest days of life. Like Isaiah, see God's greatness and love, and you will find joy in the midst of the moral decadence around you.

Christ's Suffering and Death

"Many were amazed when they saw him. His face was so disfigured he seemed hardly human, and from his appearance, one would scarcely know he was a man... He was despised and rejected—a man of sorrows, acquainted with deepest grief. Yet it was our weaknesses he carried; it was our sorrows that weighed him down...he was pierced for our rebellion, crushed for our sins. He was beaten, so we

---

[27] NIV Study Bible, Introduction to Isaiah.

could be whole. He was whipped, so we could be healed. All of us, like sheep, have strayed away. We have left God's paths to follow our own. Yet the Lord laid on him the sins of us all." (Is. 52:14-53:3-6 NLT).

"Unjustly condemned, he was led away. No one cared... that his life was cut short... He had done no wrong and had never deceived anyone. But he was buried like a criminal; he was put in a rich man's grave.... When his life is made an offering for sin, he will have many descendants... the Lord's good plan will prosper in his hands... Because of his experience, my righteous servant will make it possible for many to be counted righteous, for he will bear all their sins." (53:8-12 NLT).

True Fasting

"Declare to my people their rebellion... On the day of your fasting, you exploit all your workers. Your fasting ends in quarreling and strife, and in striking each other with wicked fists... Is not this the kind of fast I have chosen: to loosen the chains of injustice... to set the oppressed free and break every yoke? Is it not to share your food with the hungry and to provide the poor wanderer with shelter... Then your light will break forth like the dawn and your healing will quickly appear... Then you will call and the Lord will answer, you will cry for help, and he will say, 'Here am I'" (Is. 58:1-9).

They were "church-going" people, but their lives were far from what their worship represented. We have become comfortable with worldliness. When have you had a sincere discussion of what it means to be a disciple? The praise of men is more important than the smile of God. Where are the Christians who have a passion for holiness and obedience? It's not pietism, legalism, or fundamentalism to take holiness seriously. It's the way of all those called to live a life of holiness by a holy God.

JEREMIAH

Man of Passion

JEREMIAH 20:7-9

Have you ever felt like just giving up—feeling everyone is against you? God had sent Micah, Isaiah and Zephaniah to Israel in the north to warn them concerning their idolatrous behavior, but they paid no attention. As a consequence, they were exiled to Assyria. God called Jeremiah to the south because Judah was blindly following in Israel's wickedness. Unless they repented, the nation would now be faced with famine and starvation. Invaders would plunder and take them captive to Babylon. (Jer. 14:12; 15:1-4; 16:4-10).

Imagine God calling you as a teen to warn your family and relatives of a dreadful future. Scholars believe Jeremiah was seventeen years old when God gave him the assignment to tell his people how horrible conditions would be in the near future unless they repented. They would be taken captive to Babylon for a period of seventy years. Jeremiah announced that repentance is their only hope to avoid disaster. (Jer. 25:11-12; 29:10-11). God says, 'Obey me and I will be your God and you will be my people'" If you do not follow other gods...then I will let you live in this place... (Jer. 7:5-7, 23).

God Calls Youth

God frequently calls youth. Samuel was young when God called him. Probably the disciples were in their teens or early twenties when Jesus called them. On youth Sunday, I had a young man of sixteen-years-old bring the morning message. Now he is a missionary in Africa. God calls all of us, regardless of our age, to a life of service. Let's not overlook his call to our youth. Have you ever looked a young person in the eyes and said, "I can see you functioning in a particular vocation? We need Christians in that field. I believe you would do well."

Does your church intentionally involve youth, giving them some responsibility? Many churches would rather die than give up their control. Are you willing to walk beside and mentor your youth and gradually let them take some responsibility? Few Christians are willing to spend time walking with their youth, discipling them as Jesus did with his disciples. This needs to happen in order for them to become disciples who make disciples.

The Weeping Prophet

Jeremiah exposed the sins of the people: adultery, oppressing the foreigners, orphans and widows (Jer. 5:7-9; 7:5-9); lying and slander (Jer. 9:4-6). "No one repents of his wickedness, saying, 'What have I done?' Each pursues his own course... My people do not know the requirements of the Lord... I will give their wives to other men and their fields to new owners... Prophets and priests alike all practice deceit... Are they ashamed of their loathsome conduct? No, they have no shame at all; they do not even know how to blush... says the Lord..." (Jer. 8:6-12).

Jeremiah wept because he saw what was happening to his people. He felt God's pain, and his heart was broken for his people. Despite all his efforts, the people would not listen. Jeremiah was lonely. He had no support from family because God had forbidden him to marry and have children (Jer. 16:2). His friends turned their backs on him.

Have you ever wept for your family and friends because they are choosing the wrong path? Jeremiah pours out his heart to God, not once, but throughout his life. What God feels—he feels. He weeps for his people on behalf of God. He not only proclaims God's message he embodies the message. He weeps because no one will listen.

Jesus Weeps

When Jesus came riding into Jerusalem on a colt the crowds were rejoicing because they saw him as their conquering king—a national political hero. Jesus wept because the crowds completely misunderstood his mission. Jesus' focus was on another kingdom—a kingdom of peace. Jesus weeps out of empathy, not anger. He loves people—each one is precious. He wants the best for them, but they don't understand him. He knew that in a few days the crowds would turn on him executing him as a criminal.

Jesus expresses his compassion for people. In Luke 13:34 he prays, "O Jerusalem, Jerusalem, the city that kills the prophets and stones those sent to her! How often I wanted to gather your children together, just as a hen gathers her brood under her wings, and you would not have it." Less than 40 years later; in AD 70 more than 1,000,000 residents of Jerusalem died in one of the most gruesome sieges in recorded history. If you weep because of your concern for people, you are in good company with Jeremiah and Jesus. Jesus wept for lost people. Do you and I weep for our lost friends?

Like Jeremiah, Jesus often withdrew to pray and cry for the lost that he wanted to rescue, i.e. tears for the destitute, lonely and broken and poor that need a Savior. But unlike Jeremiah, Jesus himself is the answer.

"During the days of Jesus' life on earth, he offered up prayers and petitions with loud cries and tears to the one who could save him from death, and he was heard because of his reverent submission." (Heb. 5:7). Jesus wept because of the indescribable agony of taking my sin and the sin of the world upon himself. God heard and saved Jesus from eternal death by raising him to life.

God is looking for sincere people who will love him with all their heart, soul, mind and strength. A. W. Tozer said, "The only fear I have is to fear I may get out of the will of God. Outside of the will of God, there's nothing I want, and in the will of God, there's nothing I fear."

Until our passion is burning hot and we shed tears for our family, churches and our communities, America will continue its moral skid. In my fifty years of pastoring I have found that no other subject seems to run off, like water on a duck's back as prayer. Announce a prayer meeting and you will not need to look for additional chairs. Lord, teach (me) us to pray.

Jeremiah's people had become so hardened by sin they no longer feared God. We are close behind. Jeremiah preached for 40 years, and not once did he see any real success in changing or softening the hearts and minds of these stubborn, idolatrous people. Perhaps Jesus would call this, "casting your pearls before swing.

Persecution

Jeremiah's message aroused great hostility and even death threats. (Jer. 11:21). He was a laughingstock to the people and a target of mockery (Jer. 12: 6-7). His own relatives betrayed him. He was beaten and put in the stocks. Later he was put into a cistern, and sank into the mud (Jer. 20:1-2, 38:1-13). But God promised Jeremiah he would make him as a fortified bronze wall because they will fight against you but you will prevail. (Jer. 15:20-21).

Perhaps an even greater pain was his emotional suffering. "Since my people are crushed, I am crushed; I mourn, and horror grips me... Is there no physician?... I would weep day and night for the slain of my people... Every brother is a deceiver, and every friend a slanderer... no one speaks the truth... they weary themselves with sinning... They have followed the stubbornness of their hearts." (8:21-9:5, 14). If Jeremiah could find one honest person in Jerusalem, God would spare the city. (Jer. 5:1). "The mothers and fathers will die of deadly diseases..." (16:3-4). The people of Judah built high places for Baal... to sacrifice their sons and daughters to Moloch." (Jer. 32:35). Jeremiah was accused of treason. The king ordered Jeremiah to be beaten and thrown in prison, where he remained a long time. (Jer. 37:11-16).

Thousands of Christians today are imprisoned for their faith. The OpenDoor website reports: "According to The Pew Research Center, over 75% of the world's population lives in areas with severe religious restrictions (and many of these people are Christians). According to the United States Department of State, Christians in more than 60 countries face persecution from their governments or surrounding neighbors simply because of their belief in Jesus Christ." We may never face persecution as Jeremiah or suffer under a repressive government, but we need to be prepared to suffer as they suffer. Perhaps persecution is the only way for American Christians to become zealous for the Lord.

Discouragement

Jeremiah tried to make the people understand their problem was a lack of belief, trust, and faith in God. They were blindly taking

God for granted. It is easy to be lulled into a false sense of security. They replaced God with false gods, those that would not make them feel guilty or convict them of sin.

Jeremiah experienced discouragement. But God was not done with him. Jeremiah 15:19 records a lesson for each believer to remember in those times when they feel alone, useless, and discouraged and their faith is wavering: "Therefore this is what the LORD says: 'If you repent, I will restore you that you may serve me; if you utter worthy, not worthless, words, you will be my spokesman. Let this people turn to you, but you must not turn to them.'" God says to Jeremiah, come back to me, and I will restore to you the joy of your salvation. We too become discouraged when we make repeated efforts to warn our friends who ignore us.

This great prophet, Jeremiah, experienced rejection, depression, and discouragement. This is normal. We usually grow in baby steps, that's why maturity takes years and even decades.

God says that the time will come when people will not tolerate the truth (II Tim. 4:3-4). Those in Judah were saying: "Mind your own business. I don't want to hear your message of judgment which exasperates us. Just get out of our hair." As believers, our task of warning the lost and dying world of judgment is not easy. (Rev. 3:10). God says that His warnings sound like "foolishness" to those who are lost, but to believers it is the very words of life (1 Cor. 1:18). We must persevere in proclaiming truth like Jeremiah and Jesus, even though we know that most people will not listen.

Words of Hope

God speaks words of hope to his people. God promises to protect the Jewish exiles during their stay in Babylon and cause them to return to Judah after 70 years (Jer. 25:11-12; 29:5-10; 33:6-7). "The time will come when I will heal Jerusalem's wounds and give it prosperity and true peace. I will restore the fortunes of Judah and Israel and rebuild their towns. I will cleanse them of their sins... and forgive all their sins of rebellion." (Jer. 3:6-8 NLT). God also gave the encouraging promise of restoration in his coming messianic Kingdom (Jer. 23:3-8).

God will bring a remnant back to Judah to rebuild Jerusalem and the temple (Jer. 29:10-14; 30:2-3). In reference to Jesus, God will raise up a descendant of David to serve him and guide His people. (Jer. 23:5-6; 33:14-17). In fact, God would bring a remnant back to Israel a second time bringing unity to his people healing their spiritual wounds. (Jer. 3:18; 16:14-15; 23:7-8).

Today we have Good News. Jesus sent his Holy Spirit to live in us. Two hundred times in the New Testament we are reminded that God's dwelling place is in our hearts. We are a new creation in Christ Jesus, partakers with his very nature. (II Cor. 5:17, II Peter 1:4). We are free from condemnation and are more than conquerors. (Ro. 8:1, 36-39). 20 Msg.).

Prophets Needed Today

God is merciful and long-suffering in dealing with the sins and ignorance of men, but He will not leave the guilty unpunished. (Exodus 34:6-7). "The people of Judah and Jerusalem had made the Lord so angry that he finally turned his back on them" (II Kings 24:19 CEV).

Prior to their captivity, God told the people of Judah: "For I know the plans I have for you, declares the Lord, plans to prosper you and not to harm you, plans to give you hope and a future. Then you will call upon me and come and pray to me, and I will listen to you. You will seek me and find me when you seek me with all you heart" (Jer. 29:11-13).

Jeremiah was inspired to look beyond the distressing scenes of the present to the hope of a glorious future. (Jer. 31:12). A new day is promised, "I will give them a heart to know Me, that I am the LORD; and they shall be My people, and I will be their God, for they shall return to Me with all their heart" (Jer. 24:7). The final fulfillment will come when Jesus Christ returns to establish the Kingdom of God.

A Flaming Fire

After the Book of the Law was discovered Jeremiah devoted himself to preaching "the words of this covenant" to the people. (Jer. 11:1-14). Jeremiah tells God, "I am ridiculed all day long; everyone mocks me. Whenever I speak, I cry out proclaiming violence and destruction. So, the word of the Lord has brought me insult and reproach all day long. But if I say, 'I will not mention him or speak any more in his name,' his word is in my heart like a fire, a fire shut up in my bones. I am weary of holding it in; indeed, I cannot" (Jer. 20:7-9).

Are you aware of prophets today to whom God's word is like a flaming fire in their heart? Pray for God to raise up prophets who can withstand the rejection of their message.

Jeremiah had to confront the false prophets with their drugs and witchcraft. "Prophets are prophesying to you false visions, divinations, idolatries and the delusion of their own minds" (Jer. 14:14). The root word for pharmacy is "pharmakia. It means the general illicit use of drugs to cast spells, etc. (Gal. 5:20). Illicit drugs are killing thousands today. Our suicide rate continues to climb especially among our youth. The National Institute of Drug Abuse reports 72,000 deaths from overdose of drugs.

Social media and TV absorb several hours a day. The degeneration of the family, increasing violence, pornography, the acceptance of homosexual lifestyles, greed, lack of honesty and total ignorance of God's Word are issues that present a passionate call for God to raise up prophets.

Jeremiah's task was tremendously challenging. The people loved to listen to the false prophets (Jer. 5:31). Is this not a picture of our American Christianity who love to listen to the hyper-grace messages? "Hyper-grace preachers today choose to emphasize only God's love and forgiveness while practically ignoring Jesus' call for His people to walk in wholehearted commitment to the Lord. They preach mostly on forgiveness without repentance and on receiving God's blessing on their circumstances without any conditions. The truth is, it's glorious that we are freely forgiven by Jesus and that He blesses our circumstance; but these truths are in context to seeking to live in a real relationship with Him and in agreement with His leadership and Word."

What message is God calling you to give? When is the last time you heard the word "sin"? Is "sin" ever mentioned in our public-school classrooms? "My people have committed two sins: They have forsaken me, the spring of living water, and have dug their own cisterns, broken cisterns that cannot hold water" (Jer. 2:13). How true of American culture today! America is turning its back on God.

Jeremiah's Strong Faith

"The Lord's kindness never fails! If he had not been merciful, we would have been destroyed. The Lord can always be trusted to show mercy each morning. Deep in my heart I say, 'The Lord is all I need; I can depend on him!'" (Lamentations 3:22-24 CEV).

AMOS

A Prophet for the Poor

Amos comes on the scene when both society and faith were bankrupt. Unlike Isaiah who moved among kings, God chose a "poor man" to speak to the rich and affluent people of Israel. Amos was a farmer who understood the common people of Israel and Judah. He was at the bottom of the social ladder. He defended the poor and confronted the powerful rich who used God's name to legitimize their sins. If you feel that God can't use you because you don't have money or a college degree, consider Amos.

Amos was a lowly shepherd, like David, a keeper of sheep. Shepherds had a history of being despised. When Jacob and his family came to Egypt, the "Egyptians did not want to be around anyone who raised sheep" (Gen.46:34 CEV). Since Amos lived in the fields, he could not wash his hands before each meal which meant he was unclean according to the Jewish laws and traditions. Being a shepherd meant he was not permitted to enter the temple or be a witness in court.

When Jesus was born, the angels first appeared to the despised, "unclean" shepherds in the field with the good news of his birth. Jesus' incarnation underscores God's "upside-down" Kingdom. Jesus had no place to lay his head. (Matt. 8:20). He had no possession except the clothes on his back. He was a refugee. (Matt. 2:13-15). When he called his disciples, he called several fishermen like Simon, Andrew, James and John. Jesus died a poor man and so did all of his disciples.

At the beginning of Jesus' public ministry, he stood up in the synagogue and read from Isaiah 61:1-2, "The Spirit of the Lord is on me, because he has anointed me to proclaim good news to the poor... freedom for the prisoners... recovery of sight for the blind, to set the oppressed free..." (Luke 4:18-19). When John the Baptist was in prison, he questioned if Jesus was truly the Messiah. Jesus said tell John, "The Good News is being proclaimed to the poor" (Matt. 11:5).

Jesus joined those at the bottom, the outcasts and undesirables. Jesus invites us into a journey of downward mobility, so we can understand and win those on the margins as he did.

Since the desire to be rich separates us from himself and from the poor, Jesus spoke more about the evils of money than any other subject. He knew money can so easily become our god. Jesus' brother, James says, "God has chosen those who are poor in the eyes of the world to be rich in faith and to inherit the kingdom he promised those who love him" (James 2:5). Paul reminds us that few whom God calls are... influential or of noble birth. But God chose the foolish things of the world, the weak things to shame the strong, the lowly things and the despised things, so no one can boast about their abilities. (I Cor. 1:26-29).

While Amos was a keeper of sheep, he was fully aware of the conditions of the surrounding nations as he traded with the caravans of merchants who needed to travel through this barren terrain to trade their fair. He traveled from Judah and journeyed twenty-two miles to Bethel in the Northern Kingdom as God's messenger to his neighbors in Israel.

After Amos identifies himself, (1:1) he immediately launches into warning the surrounding nations of God's judgment on their sin. "The Lord roars from Zion and thunders from Jerusalem" (v. 2). He moves rapidly through Damascus, Gaza, Tyre, Edom, Ammon, Moab. Judah and Israel must have rejoiced when they heard what God was going to do with their enemies. (Chapters 1 and 2). But from this point to midway through the final chapter, (9:7), he brings his warning home to Judah and Israel. His message was so powerful that Amaziah, the priest, tried to stop Amos from preaching. (7:10-13). The book concludes with a clear message of hope: God will restore his people and make them great again. (9:7-15).

Parallels of Israel and America

Amos's message fits closely with our American situation. Israel and Judah were in a time of prosperity with people living in luxury while the poor were treated as slaves. Try to imagine a prophet like Amos coming to America today. Amos begins with announcing judgment on Damascus, the capitol of Syria to the north.

Damascus, used its threshing tools to drag over the back of their enemies just like they used those tools to drag over the grain at harvest time. (1:3). Too many Americans, filled with revenge, use their guns and knives in mass killings which now averages one every day. (A mass killing occurs when four or more people are killed). Our homicide rate continues to climb.

The people of Israel, "sell the righteous for silver and the needy for a pair of sandals" (2:6). The 2017 human trafficking statistics as reported by the National Human Trafficking Hotline reveals 8,759 cases of human trafficking reported to the NHTH, representing over 10,000 individual victims, almost 5,000 potential traffickers, and more than 1,500 businesses involved in human trafficking." Sex trafficking is now called, "The New American Slavery." There are a million prostitutes in our nation.

"A father and son use the same girl and so profane my holy name" (2:7b). America has led many nations astray by Hollywood's morality, promoting pornography, homosexuality and sex outside of marriage which we unashamedly and blazingly portray in our movies and public media around the world.

The people, "trample on the head of the poor as upon the dust of the ground and deny justice to the oppressed" (2:7a). We are one of the richest nations of the world, but there are 39.7 million Americans living in poverty, fifteen million are children.

The people of Ammon ripped open pregnant women, so they could extend their border" (1:13). Abortion has become a $1.5 billion industry in America in spite of the fact that science proves that life begins at conception.

The people of Moab burned to lime the bones of the king of Edom. (Amos 2:1). There was total disrespect for rulers and for the law. Violent animosity expressed in many of our demonstrations today, if continued, will lead to the destruction of our nation.

Judah "rejected the law of the Lord, and did not keep his decrees, because they were led astray by false gods" (2:4). The Israelites practiced a fake religion. There was no connection between worship and morality. They had a form of godliness that meant nothing. "I can't stand your religious meetings, I'm fed up with your conferences and conventions. I want nothing to do with your religious projects, your pretentious slogans and goals. I'm sick of your fund-raising schemes, your public relations and image making. I've had all I can take of your noisy ego-music... Do you know what I want? I want justice - oceans of it. I want fairness—rivers of it" (Amos 5:21-24 Msg).

A Direct Message

Amos gives a scathing message to his rich neighbors. God says, "I will tear down the winter house along with the summer house; the houses adorned with ivory will be destroyed and the mansions will be demolished. Hear this word... you women who oppress the poor and crush the needy and say to your husbands, 'bring us some drinks!'... You will be taken away with hooks and be cast out" (Amos 3:15—4:3).

"It was a time of unprecedented prosperity. Wealth abounded and the people gave themselves over to a life of luxury and self-indulgence. Winter houses and summer houses with plenty of hewn stone and ivory paneling were found among the wealthy citizens. Business was good, wine was plentiful, ivory couches and rich furnishing were provided along with delicacies and stirring music for the feasts and banquets. Ease and extravagance contrasted with the misery and suffering of the slave population who could not afford the bare necessities of life. The merchant class made the money and took possession of the land which fell to the hands of a few. The judges were dishonest; the government was corrupt. Usury, extortion, riots, and class hatreds were visible on every hand. Along with all of this was found a shallow optimism that seemed utterly oblivious to the tragic certainties just around the corner."[28]

Don't Neglect the Poor

"The Lord said, 'You people crush those in need and wipe out the poor. You say to yourselves... 'our wheat is ready to sell. We can't wait to cheat, and charge high prices for the grain. We will use dishonest scales and mix dust in the grain. Those who are needy and poor don't have any money. We will make them our slaves for the price of a pair of sandals.'" (Amos 8:4-6 CEV).

---

[28] Kyle Yates, *Preaching from the Prophets*, Broadman, 1942, p. 34.

There are nearly 4,000 Scripture passages in the Bible demonstrating God's concern for orphans, widows, prisoners, immigrants, homeless, the poor, the hungry, disabled, and sick. Jesus spent considerable time with the poor.

Two Percent of Christians Know the Homeless

One survey reveals that only two percent of Christians in the United States work with or even know the poor and homeless. Most Christians do not have an in-depth relationship with anyone on the margins. Christians tend to isolate themselves from the poor. The majority of Sundays in my fifty years of pastoral ministry, I provided transportation for people who had no other way to church. This was true even in some middle-income communities. Those on the margins can be found in most every town even if it is affluent.

Multitudes on the margins have been left behind, as those who are more affluent move to the suburbs away from the crime, poverty and poor schools. We cut ourselves off from those Jesus said we are to invite to his heavenly banquet. Jesus said we are not to invite our families or anyone who can invite us back like our rich neighbors, but rather to invite those we know who cannot return the invitation. (Lk. 14:21-24). Do you have room at your Thanksgiving or Christmas meal for a poor person?

If many of our churches would have stayed in the inner city rather than moved to suburbia, our churches would be lighthouses in places where the streets are now full of poor housing, drug trafficking and crime.

The Philippian Church—Joy

The church in Philippi was the most joyful of the New Testament churches. I believe there is a direct relationship with their joy and the makeup of their church. Lydia, their first member, was a wealthy foreign woman. The second member was a formerly possessed, fortune-telling slave girl at the bottom of the social scale. The third was a common laborer, a jailer posted to guard the town's prison together with his family. (Ac. 16). There is a special joy and a greater moving of God's Spirit found in congregations where there is a variety of cultures and persons of differing economic strata. Homogeneous congregations are usually ingrown and provincial even though they may have a great foreign mission's budget. It is very unusual for a person in the lower income bracket or a different race to become a respected member in many of our churches. If you bring a person to church from a different economic status, they usually leave because they know they will not be accepted into the inner circle. This can only be overcome when we make the first thing the first thing, which is to love the Lord with all our heart and love our neighbor as Jesus loved us.

We say, "I have a spare bedroom but it's not practical at this time in my life to take in this lady with her two toddlers who has no place to go." Fifty years ago, we did not expect each child to have their own room. The average size of our house has double or tripled over the past 50 years. Maintaining a family in our present family structure makes it unlikely that other people's needs will ever be met. The desire for comfort and privacy strangles our effectiveness in God's Kingdom. We care more about the feeding of our pets than about the children who go to bed hungry. Few of our neighbor children know the true meaning of Christmas or Easter.

The Prosperity "Gospel"

The Prosperity Gospel which is so prevalent today overemphasizes God's promises of material blessings. God wants us to prosper spiritually but not necessarily materially. It's a false gospel with a focus on this world. (I John 2:15). Jesus did not come to make us comfortable, he came to make us holy, as he is holy. He came not to make us good but to make us godly.

Scripture and church history indicate that prosperity leads us to depend on ourselves rather than on God, which results in carnal living. Jesus said, "It's terribly hard for rich people to get into the kingdom of heaven! In fact, it's easier for a camel to go through the eye of a needle than for a rich person to get into God's kingdom" (Matt. 19:23-24 CEV).

Again, Jesus said, "Life does not consist of an abundance of possessions." (Lk.12:14). Jesus did not die to make us rich in this world's goods. (II Cor. 8:9). We are to seek his Kingdom above everything else and God will give us what is best for us. His wealth for us may not be riches. (Matt. 6:33). "If any of you wants to be my follower, you must turn from your selfish ways, take up your cross, and follow me. If you try to hang on to your life, you will lose it. But if you give up your life for my sake and for the sake of the Good News, you will save it. And what do you benefit if you gain the whole world but lose your own soul? Is anything worth more than your soul?" (Mark 8:34-37). The Prosperity Gospel is more self-gratification than the self-denial Jesus demands of his disciples.

Prosperity proponents teach that everyone can be rich if we have faith. Do the prosperity proponents take this message to the millions in India, Nigeria, Mozambique, Congo and Bangladesh? When they do, they give a false hope. They focus on wealth rather than God's faithfulness in times of suffering and poverty. Paul understood this when he wrote, "We are poor but make many rich." (II Cor. 6:10).

"Godliness with contentment is great gain... If we have food and clothing, we will be content with that... For the love of money is a root of all kinds of evil. Some people eager for money, have wandered from the faith and pierced themselves with many griefs" (I Tim. 6:6-10).

"It is a great principle with George Muller that it does not become the children of God to be ostentatious in style, appointment, dress, or manner of living. He believes that expensiveness and luxury are not seemly in those who are the professed disciples of the meek and lowly One who had no place to lay his head." A college president chooses to live frugally. He lives simply so that others can simply live. More than half the people of the world have never spoken on a phone. Do we shut our eyes and hearts to them?

Those on the margins are often more receptive to the Good News because of their need for love and acceptance. In the parable of the great banquet, the rich were deaf to God's invitation while the poor were glad to come. The master sent his servants to invite the guests but they all made excuses: one just got married, another bought real estate, and yet another purchased farm equipment. The master was angry and told his servants to bring in the poor, the crippled, the blind and the lame, but there was still room. The master said, "Go out to the road and country lanes and make them come in, so that my house will be full. I tell you, not one of those men who were invited will get a taste of my banquet" (Luke 14:15-24).

A woman said to me, "I've been praying and witnessing to my neighbor for twenty years. She does not seem to be one step closer to God." She described her friend as having a lucrative job, excellent health and a nice house. Two suggestions: first, pray for God to bring into her life whatever it takes to wake her up. That sounds cruel, but wouldn't we rather see her suffer for a few years than spend eternity in hell? Many Christians don't believe in hell which naturally takes away their passion to win people for Christ. Secondly, perhaps you need to "shake the dust off your feet" and seek others who are more receptive. (Lk. 10:11). There are multitudes all around you who need Jesus.

To prosperity proponents, God is a bellhop responding to our desires. Life is me-centered rather than God centered. Faith becomes the servant to make God do what we desire. Rather we must be God servants, we don't tell God what to do. Prosperity people seldom mention the necessity of holiness. (Heb. 12:14). The fruit of the Spirit is not wealth, but love, joy, peace, patience, etc. (Gal. 5:22-23).

Love the Poor

To show and model God's love, we have to get close to those we serve, even when it isn't comfortable. Paul says he became all things to all people to win them to Christ. (I Cor. 9:22). Working with people on the margins, you may find yourself cleaning up vomit, dealing with bugs and offensive smells of all kinds. When you hug a smelly person, you will pick up their scent, but they will also pick up the fragrance of Jesus from you. I relate closely to several men who have come off alcohol and drugs. It's encouraging to see them growing in faith. Invading the devil's territory is never easy. It's tiring spiritually, emotionally, mentally and physically. (I Thess. 3:5; Gal. 4:11). Those on the margins have been deeply wounded. Only love in action will reach them. There is no expansion of God's Kingdom without costly sacrificial love and service.

One of my dear friends was born in extreme poverty. As a little boy, he had to walk barefoot a couple miles to church. Today he is head of a large Christian mission, overseeing a hundred or more missionaries in thirty countries. Remember, Joseph was a slave, Moses and David were shepherds, Gideon and Amos were farmers, Jephthah was the son of a prostitute. Hannah was a homemaker and Esther an orphan girl. God used them and he will use you!

Can the Rich Enter Heaven?

You may ask, "Can a rich person enter heaven?" Levi and Zacchaeus were wealthy tax collectors. Lydia was a wealthy business woman. Jesus said it is hard for the rich to enter heaven but with God all things are possible. (Matt. 19:23-24). Paul instructs Pastor Timothy, "Command those who are rich in this present world not to be arrogant nor to put their hope in wealth, which is so uncertain, but to put their hope in God, who richly provides us with everything for our enjoyment. Command them to do good, to be rich in good deeds, and to be generous and willing to share. In this way they will lay up treasure for themselves as a firm foundation for the coming age, so that they may take hold of the life that is truly life" (I Tim. 6:17-19).

Whether rich or poor, man or woman, educated or uneducated, God will use you to the extent that you give your allegiance to him. Most of the rapidly growing churches in the world today are in third world countries where many of the church leaders are learning to read and write. We are all created in God's image. Anyone he created can be a tool, an instrument in God's hand if they yield their allegiance to him.

Amos towers as defender of the poor and the downtrodden. "You, Lord God, bless everyone who cares for the poor" (Psalm 41:1 CEV). To the rich young ruler who believed he had obeyed all the commandments, Jesus said, "If you want to be perfect, go sell everything you own! Give the money to the poor, and you will have riches in heaven. Then come and be my follower" (Matt. 19:21 CEV). Will you take time to learn the names of the poor around you, listen to their pain and show God's love to them?

God's Everlasting Love to His People.

What a great future awaits God's faithful children! "You will have such a harvest that you won't be able to bring in all of your wheat before the plowing time. You will have grapes left over from season to season; your fruitful vineyards will cover the mountains. I'll make Israel prosper again. You will rebuild your towns and live in them. You will drink wine from your own vineyards and eat the fruit you grow. I'll plant your roots deep in the land I have given you, and you won't ever be uprooted again. I, the Lord God, have spoken!" (Amos 9:13-15).

We Will Be With Jesus

"We know that when Jesus appears, we shall be like him, for we shall see him as he is. Everyone who has this hope in him purifies himself, just as he is pure" (I John 3:2-3). You can't live any better than that! Even so come Lord Jesus!

JONAH

The Reluctant Prophet

There are good prophets and not so good prophets. Jonah was not a false prophet but an unwilling prophet. He was averse to doing what God called him to do.

The Lord told Jonah: "Get up and go to the great city of Nineveh! Announce my judgment against it because I have seen how wicked its people are… But Jonah got up and went in the opposite direction in order to get away from the Lord. He went down to the sea coast, to the port of Joppa, where he found a ship leaving for Tarshish. He bought a ticket and went on board, hoping that by going away to the west he could escape from the Lord" (Jonah 1:2-3 NLT).

How often has the Lord asked you to say something or do something and you chose to go in the opposite direction or you drug your feet? You know Jesus said, "as the Father sent Jesus so he sends you" (John 17:18). Have you lived beside your neighbor for years or worked beside your peers and never took the opportunity to share your faith? Have you sat beside an unsaved friend in class for a semester and never prayed for them or let them know where you stand on a moral issue and why you hold to this belief?

Joe a golfer, invited Sam to go golfing Sunday morning. Sam said, "Sunday I'm in church." Joe said, "Give up that nonsense. You know you don't believe it." Sam replied, "What do you mean?" "I can prove you don't believe," replied Joe. "I worked with you every day for twenty years. The Bible says that I'm headed for hell but you were never concerned enough to urge me to consider changing my life." Ask yourself: "Am I like Sam?"

Do those you associate with know you are a follower of Jesus? Since Jesus commissioned or mandated us to share the Gospel, we have a responsibility to not only live our faith but to proclaim our faith in word and deed. (Matt. 28:18-20; Acts 1:8). I pray every day for that the Lord will open my eyes to those who might be receptive to hearing the eternal Word of faith. Even the expression, "Have a good day. God bless you," can remind people that God is present. It is a joy to experience the Spirit's leading daily as I mention God and his goodness. If I come to the end of the day and have not moved someone closer to Jesus, I ask God to forgive me for not seeing an opportunity to share him. Ask Jesus to open your eyes to see the opportunities to share your faith. Pray for courage and Holy Spirit boldness to speak with a gentle but confident word of God's grace and love. Jesus said, "I did not speak of my own accord, but the Father who sent me commanded me what to say and how to say it" (John 12:49). I also pray every day that I will speak only what the Father wants me to say and to guide me how to say it. Our tone of voice reveals our heart and is often more important than what we say. Jesus will give you the words to say if you ask him. Be sure your life is lined up with your message.

You Are God's Representative

Living with an awareness that you are God's representative will help you be more conscious of listening for his voice. You will experience joy on a level you didn't know was possible. (John 15:11). "Whoever claims to live in him must walk as Jesus did" (I John 2:6). "In this world we are like him" (I John 4:17). You are Jesus to people. As our culture becomes more and more pagan, you will meet people every day who have no idea what's in the bible because they have never read the bible. The younger generation has no understanding of the meaning of Christmas or Easter. They cannot tell the difference between the Old Testament or the New Testament or give you the name of a gospel or an apostle. Any response on their part of criticism of the bible can be met with the loving question: "Have you ever read the bible?"

God Gets Jonah's Attention

God sent a storm in an effort to open Jonah's eyes. "All the sailors were afraid and each cried out to his own god. And they threw the cargo into the sea to lighten the ship. But Jonah had gone below deck, where he lay down and fell into a deep sleep" (Jonah 1:5). In the next chapter Jonah awoke and said, "As my life was slipping away, I remembered the Lord and my earnest prayer went out to you in your holy temple." (2:7). In the final two chapters Jonah reluctantly goes to Nineveh with God's message. When they repent, Jonah is angry because of God's forgiveness to the wicked Ninevites. When you hear of a "wicked" person's transformation, do you feel God is unfair or do you rejoice at their conversion? God made a plant to shade Jonah and then prepared a worm to eat the plant and ordered a scorching wind to blow on Jonah. Jonah is so frustrated and depressed he wishes he could die.

"The Lord said, 'You feel sorry about the plant, though you did nothing to put it there. It came quickly and died quickly. But Nineveh has more than 120,000 people living in spiritual darkness, not to mention all the animals. Shouldn't I feel sorry for such a great city?'" (4:10-11 NLT).

God often has to take us to "the belly of a fish" where we become desperate so we wake up and cry out to him. The sailors facing great danger cried out to their god(s) in desperation. Jonah was desperate in the belly of that great fish. God allows us to go through heart-breaking tragedies like Jonah and the sailors. God designed these tragedies to get our attention, to wake us up and soften our hearts so we come to him for help and healing. Are you going through a trial now: perhaps the death of a loved one, a health crisis or financial crisis, the rejection of a spouse or a family member or a friend?

Desperation Drives Us to Focus on the Eternal

These sailors go to great lengths to avoid disaster, even throwing their cargo into the sea, their paychecks were gone. People today go to great lengths to suppress and try to cover up their emptiness. They long for purpose and satisfaction. They frantically chase after their god(s) not aware of what or why they are doing so. Multitudes in America have made money their god. They spend increditable amounts of money and time on movies, sports, the latest model iPhone, bigger TV screen, travel, casinos, party lifestyle, drugs, alcohol, cigarettes and larger houses. They work extra hours, neglecting their family. Children are forced to raise themselves, marriages breakup, others are not married but have children to several partners.

It is no surprise our social workers are overloaded and our prisons are overflowing.

Many live with a shipload of fear that their gods won't come through, so they work all the harder. They keep themselves busy deliberately, intentionally trying to silence God's voice. They give their time to things/gods of the world. They know more about movie heroes than they do about Jesus. They travel to see the sites in God's spectacular world but give no thought of God who created them. They see the new born baby and assume it is just nature doing its normal thing. No thought or thankfulness is given to God. They may see a kind act and think, "that's good," but their schedules are too full to help others with acts of kindness.

Have You Fallen Asleep?

We see and hear accounts of suffering people every day. Don't allow yourself to become hardened like Jonah who fell asleep ignoring people's cry for help. Our conscience has become seared. (I Tim. 4:2). Our hearts have become hardened. Jonah focused on the godless lifestyle on the Ninevites rather than seeing them as persons created in God's image in need of God's grace. When one of your "enemies" is transformed by God's love, is your first thought, "How wonderful that they found new life?" Or is your first thought, "That's not fair. They don't deserve God's love and forgiveness for all the wicked things they have done?" Are we rejoicing today as thousands of Muslims are coming to faith in Christ? Are we like Jonah, hostile to people who are different than us or are a threat to our security? All churches say, "You are welcome." For most churches that is not true. Are prisoners or those on parole welcome? What about the depressed, the homeless, the drug addicts, the alcoholics? Do you flinch at cigarette butts outside your church door? What about the single mother with her children? Do you take time to befriend them, invite them to your dinner table or are we like Jonah, asleep in a pew?

We know God is not willing that any should perish. Why are Christians often reluctant to welcome the unchurched? Are we afraid our children will adopt their lifestyle? Whenever those thoughts enter our minds, we are saying, "Our God is anemic. He is not adequate to keep us." We know that God loves the people of the world. We know we are sent like Jonah to our adversaries. Have we lost faith to believe those in the world can change so we do nothing? Are we relieved when we hear they went to another church?

Why was Jonah so adverse to seeing the Ninevites coming to God? Nineveh was a wicked city. The Ninevites were the enemy. Jonah was sucked into the religious self-righteous culture of his time. In the Jonah account, the people of Nineveh repented. They changed. The Holy Spirit is in the business of changing people's lives today. Ask God to give you a heart of compassion like Jesus who didn't exclude anyone, but gave his life freely for everyone.

I'd Rather Be a Sailor Than Be Jonah

"The sailors asked Jonah, "Tell us, who is responsible for making all this trouble for us? What do you do? Where do you come from? What is your country? From what people are you?" (1:8 NIV). After Jonah informed them who he was and who his God was, the sailors cried out to the Lord. They even tried to keep from throwing Jonah overboard. "'Pick me up and throw me into the sea,' he replied, 'and it will become calm. I know that it is my fault that this great storm has come upon you.'… "Instead, the men did their best to row back to land…" "Then they (the sailors) cried to the LORD, 'O Lord', please do not let us die for taking this man's life. Do not hold us accountable for killing an innocent man, for you, O Lord, have done as you pleased." (1:12-14).

Jonah, in his stubbornness, was willing to die rather than say "yes" to God's call to go to Nineveh. Jesus said, "Woe to you, teachers of the law and Pharisees, you hypocrites! You shut the kingdom of heaven in men's faces. You yourselves do not enter nor will you let those enter who are trying to" (Matt. 23:13-14). These sailors had a greater fear of God than Jonah did. I'd rather be a sailor, open to God's will, than a Jonah who knew God's will but ran the other way. Many parents and many churches know they are called to be a witness to their community. But, like Jonah, they have become self-absorbed and have put a wall around God's love. We lose our youth because we are unwilling to allow changes in our worship style or we condemn them for their cultural practices that are different from ours. We need to love them and model the Jesus way for them.

They may make us uncomfortable, but allow God's Spirit to give you grace to show genuine love and you will be blessed and so will they.

Jonah knew God. "The word of the Lord came to Jonah" (Jonah 1:1 NIV). Too often like Jonah, "the more we know about God," the more we become self-righteous. Many Christians know a lot about God but do not know the heart of God. (Matt. 22:37-39). Do you know God or do you know about God? Many are more concerned about working for God than they are learning to walk with God loving him with all their heart.

What Do I Do to Ensure that I Do Not Become Like Jonah?

When Jonah shared God's message, they repented, "Jonah was furious, he lost his temper. He yelled at God, 'God! I knew it—when I was back home, I knew this was going to happen! That's why I ran off to Tarshish! I knew you were sheer grace and mercy, not easily angered, rich in love, and ready at the drop of a hat to turn your plans of punishment into a program of forgiveness!'" (Jonah 4:1-2 Msg.).

In Luke 4 when Jesus announced in his home town synagogue in Nazareth that the good news was for everyone, even to the Gentiles, the Jewish people were ready to kill him.

We may not be ready to kill the evangelist who brings "Gentiles" into our church but our "anger" shows by our lack of acceptance. Go back to the cross and see again Jesus' love for you that drove him to the cruel cross. See the Father giving his only Son. See the Holy Spirit leaving heaven, coming to live in your sinful heart now being made holy. See the great cloud of witnesses, even greater than the crowds of 100,000+ at our football games, who have been faithful, many of them giving their lives for the cause of the Good News. (Heb. 13:1).

Hear the great commission of our Lord. Thank God for the power to be a witness (martyr) for the Gospel. Experience the joy of being faithful. Know that all heaven rejoices over one sinner who repents. Experience the peace of Christ, which is not like the peace of the world. Finally, pray over your "Jerusalem" as Jesus prayed and wept over those who were lost.

Father, forgive my indifferent attitude, forgive my jealousy and anger when people come to you who are different from my culture, traditions, opinions and preferences. Remove the "Jonah spirit" from me. Give me your heart of compassion. Amen.

HABAKKUK

Arguing with God

The Judean prophet, Habakkuk, was greatly perplexed concerning world events. Egypt and Babylon were fighting. King Nebuchadnezzar of Babylon drove the Egyptians back and took over the civilized world in 605 BC. Assyria too was in disarray. It's capitol, Nineveh, fell because of its moral decay. Habakkuk questioned, discussed, and negotiated with God. He spoke for himself on behalf of the people of God. We get to listen in on his dialogue. We too have questions concerning God's decisions in our world's turmoil.

Habakkuk begins his book with complaints: "Lord, how long must I beg for your help before you listen? How long before you save us from all this violence? Why do you make me watch such terrible injustice? Why do you allow violence, lawlessness, crime and cruelty to spread everywhere? Laws cannot be enforced; justice is always the loser; criminals crowd out honest people and twist the laws around." (1:2-4 CEV). His complaints sound familiar to us.

Questions Are OK

God wants us to think. He gives us minds that are full of questions: why, how, when, and where. We are given free will to use our minds in making good decisions. As I witness to people about Jesus, I am encouraged when they respond with questions. Sincere questions are healthy. If we never question, do we truly believe? Satan tries to keep us so preoccupied that we don't have time to think and meditate.

Science tells us we use only a very small fraction of our brain. Every word, every image we have ever seen is all recorded in our brain. Consider your dreams, where did they come from? When we stand before God, he will simply reveal to us our thoughts and actions which are recorded in our minds. Our only defense on the judgment day is the blood of Christ. The evidence of all our thoughts, words and actions will be shown to us leaving us defenseless apart from Jesus' blood which atones for our sin.

We are to reason with the Lord. (Isaiah 1:18). "Let us review the situation together and you can present your case to prove your innocence" (Is. 43:26 NLT). Scripture records 150 questions Jesus asked. He knew the answers, so why did he ask? Jesus wants us to use our minds. In Bible times, the mind and the heart were basically the same. Jesus said, "Out of the heart come evil thoughts..." (Matt. 15:19).

We show our care for an individual when we ask sincere questions to better understand what they are saying. To be understood is to loved. Their answers reveal their heart. Our relationship deepens. When we first meet someone on a casual basis, it is usually best not to ask "why" questions. "Why" questions tend to invade our privacy. After you know the person, "why questions," if sincerely asked, are appropriate and indicate your care. The relationship deepens through listening and learning to know one another.

Some Questions Have no Simple Answers

We all want answers, but some questions do not have simple answers. These questions arouse more questions and doubts. Habakkuk sought answers. Judah was in a time of oppression, persecution, lawlessness and immorality. He is brokenhearted for his people - why all this evil? Habakkuk took his questions to God. He found God's answers difficult to understand and accept. "As the heavens are higher than the earth, so are my ways higher than your ways and my thoughts than your thoughts" (Is. 55:9 also 40:13-14).

We listen to the news and ask, "Why is there so much pain? How long will it take to stop the killings on our streets and in our schools? When will people realize that the more guns we have in our homes, the more people will be wounded and killed? Guns indicate revenge. Paul writes, "Do not take revenge, but leave room for God's wrath for it is written: 'It is mine to avenge; I will repay,' says the Lord" (Ro. 8:19). "Don't insist on getting even; that's not for you to do. I'll do the judging," says God. "I'll take care of it" (Msg.). When will the nations realize the proliferation of nuclear weapons brings us closer to horrific pain and death?

Life Is Not Fair

Lord, why is my friend dying with cancer? Why have I lost my job? Why do dishonest people prosper? Why does he get all the credit for my hard work? It's not fair. We have no promise that life will be fair. Life is not fair. Life wasn't fair for Jesus, and it will not be fair for us because we live in a sinful, self-centered, me-first world. When difficulties come, we ask, "Why me?" Let's learn to ask, "Why not me?"

The Lord answers Habakkuk: "Look and be amazed at what's happening... I am sending the Babylonians. They are fierce and cruel - marching across the land, conquering cities and towns... Their troops are faster than leopards, more ferocious than wolves..." (1:5-11CEV).

God's answer is shocking. Habakkuk and his friends are terrorized by the Babylonians, a more wicked nation than Judah. Why would God use this wicked nation as his tool to punish his people? The wicked Babylonians were unaware they were God's tool to bring Judah back to God. King Cyrus, King Nebuchadnezzar, the Pharaoh's of Egypt did not know God was using them to discipline his people. Today, nations do not know they are carrying out God's will. The greatest rulers of our world are under his control. Nothing, yes, nothing is ever outside God's control. "The nations are like a drop in a bucket; they are regarded as dust on the scales... He brings princes to naught and reduces the rulers of this world to nothing. No sooner are they planted... when he blows on them and they wither, and a whirlwind sweep them away like chaff" (Isaiah 40:15, 23-24).

How Do We Address God?

Although questioning God, Habakkuk, shows reverence by addressing him as "Holy Lord God." He deeply respects God even though he can't understand him. God, you can't stand sin so how can you use these wicked Babylonians to judge and punish us. Don't sit by in silence while they gobble down people who are better than they are. (1:12-13).

God explains to Habakkuk that the arrogance and pride of the Babylonians will be their downfall. All evil will eventually be punished. No matter how unfair you are treated, if you yield to him, he will use the pain to refine you, (James 1:2-4). Others will notice your reaction to trouble and pain and be amazed that you do not become distressed or retaliate. "Keep a clear conscience, so that those who speak maliciously against your good behavior in Christ may be ashamed of their slander" (I Pet. 3:16 CEV and Matt. 5:16).

Patience

"The Lord said: 'I will give you my message... write it clearly. At the time I have decided my words will come true. You can trust what I say about the future. It may take a long time, but keep on waiting—it will happen! I, the Lord, refuse to accept any one who is proud. Only those who live by faith are acceptable to me.'" (2:2-4 CEV).

God explains how he will punish the Babylonians. They will be mocked with these words: "You're doomed! You stored up stolen goods and cheated others of what belonged to them. But without warning those you owe will demand payment. Then you will become a frightened victim. You robbed cities and nations everywhere on earth and murdered their people. Now those who survived will be cruel to you... You were ruthless to towns and people everywhere. Now you will be terrorized." (6-8, 17 CEV).

God reminds Habakkuk there is coming a day when those who terrorized you will be terrorized. "Look at that man, bloated by self-importance—full of himself but soul-empty. But the person in right standing before God through loyal and steady believing is fully alive, really alive" (2:4 Msg.). God's message to Habakkuk and to each one of us is to be patient, for the day is coming when the persecutors will be persecuted.

Live by Faith

This phrase, "The righteous will live by faith" (2:4) is quoted in four different books of the New Testament. "Without faith we cannot please God" (Heb. 11:6). We trust God to direct all affairs of our life as well as the affairs of the nations.

"Has not God Almighty determined that the people's labor is only fuel for the fire and that the nations exhaust themselves for nothing?" (Hab. 2:13). God says, "The earth will be filled with the knowledge of the glory of the Lord, as the waters cover the sea" (v.14). This answer trumps all our frustration. The land will be filled with people who know and honor the Lord. There is a bright and glorious day coming when all God's children will obey the Lord. Live in this promise.

Unbelievable Triumph

In Habakkuk 3:1-15, we see Habakkuk's faith rise to a new level. He prays, "Please turn from your anger and be merciful; do for us what you did for our ancestors... Your glory covered the heavens, and your praises were heard everywhere on earth... In your furious anger, you trampled on nations to rescue your people and save your chosen one. You crushed a nation's ruler and stripped his evil kingdom of its power."

With Habakkuk's intense encounter with God, he shares his feelings: "When I heard this message (from God) I felt weak from fear... my bones seemed to melt, and I stumbled around. But I will patiently wait. Someday those vicious enemies will be struck by disaster." (3:16 CEV).

Faith Soars

Habakkuk concludes his book with some of the most fantastic and challenging words in the bible. After dialoging with God, Habakkuk's faith soars too. He says, "Fig trees may no longer bloom, or vineyards produce grapes; olive trees may be fruitless, and harvest time a failure, sheep pens may be empty, and cattle stalls vacant - but I will still celebrate because the Lord God saves me. The Lord gives me strength. He makes my feet as sure as those of a deer, and he helps me stand on the mountains." (3:17-19 CEV).

Habakkuk celebrated even though the world was crumbling all around him? Put Habakkuk's confession in present day America: I lost my job. The bottom dropped out of the stock market. My savings depleted. My spouse left me with the children, and there is no food in the cupboard. The doctor tells me I have a cancerous tumor, furthermore, those all around me are discouraged and depressed.

Job practiced what Habakkuk wrote. (Job 1:13-19). In one day, four different messengers came. The first messenger informed Job that all his farm equipment was stolen, and his hired men were killed. The second messenger arrived while the first was still speaking and said that lightning storms burned all the sheep. While he was still speaking a third messenger said that the Chaldeans swept down and carried off all his camels and killed those with the camels. Finally, a fourth messenger came while the third was still speaking giving Job the news that while his children were together, a hurricane destroyed the house and no one survived. "At this, Job got up and tore his robe and shaved his head. Then he fell to the ground in worship and said: Naked I came from my mother's womb, and naked I will depart. The Lord gave and the Lord has taken away; may the name of the Lord be praised. In all this, Job did not sin by charging God with wrongdoing" (Job 1:20-22). For Paul's similar experiences see First Corinthians 4:11-13 or II Cor. 11:24-29.

Millions in today's world live in extreme poverty. Some of the most vibrant churches are found "underground" as Christians gather in little cells to worship God and encourage each other. Many are persecuted. In many of these places the church is growing. The supernatural has become natural for them. They live in Christ's resurrection power and are joyful.

My friend had chosen Habakkuk's final three verses many years ago as his life verses. While he was going through the valley of the shadow of death with cancer he rested in these verses. He died of cancer at age sixty-six. While I have never experienced the devastation described by Habakkuk, I have had some very difficult experiences in my fifty years of pastoral ministry. There were at least two experiences that involved organized rejection. In these situations, I did not turn cartwheels of joy or feel like I was king on the mountain. I had some growing to do. However, looking back, these two experiences were some of the most meaningful of my life. They changed my life's direction. They enriched me immensely. In fact, I would not be writing this book or have written any books without those experiences. I am learning to not only trust God, but to rejoice knowing God will prevail. I rejoice in God my Savior, finding that the supernatural is natural.

One of the most encouraging words of Jesus: "Blessed are you when people mock you and persecute you and lie about you and say all sorts of evil things against you because you are my followers. Be happy, be very glad! For a great reward awaits you in heaven" (Matt. 5:11-12). When experiencing these very trying times, can we rejoice in knowing our reward will be great in heaven?

Take your eyes off of your difficulties and focus on God. He will give you strength, even in the times of devastation. Jesus said, "Do not be afraid of those who can kill the body but cannot kill the soul. Rather, be afraid of the One who can destroy body and soul in hell" (Matt. 10:28).

Habakkuk said, he will rejoice in the Lord. His faith was in God. He took this message literally: The righteous will live by faith. (2:4). When your world is crumbling around you and you see no way out, look to God to give you strength and faith even though God may permit you to suffer and die. God will bring about his justice and rid the world of evil in his time. Like Jesus: "Because of the joy awaiting him, he endured the cross, disregarding its shame." (Heb. 12:2 NLT). Paul writes: "I consider that our present sufferings are not worth comparing with the glory that will be revealed in us." (Rom. 12:18). Isaiah wrote that God who created the earth "will not grow tired or weary, and his understanding no one can fathom. He gives strength to the weary and increases the power of the weak... Those who hope in the Lord will renew their strength. They will soar on wings like eagles; they will run and not grow weary, they will walk and not be faint" (Is. 40:28-31).

Why would God use the wicked, barbaric nations to punish his wayward people? Might God use terrorists, drug thugs, police states and scandals to chasten us? We must learn not to complain about the kind of discipline God chooses to use in disciplining us. He knows what is best and will bring about justice in his time. The time is coming when: "The earth will be filled with the knowledge of the glory of the Lord as the waters cover the sea." (2:14). In the mean-time, we are more than conquerors through Christ. "I am convinced that neither death nor life, neither angels nor demons, neither the present nor the future, nor any powers, neither height nor depth, nor anything else in all creation, will be able to separate us from the love of God that is in Christ Jesus our Lord." (Romans 8:38-39).

With God's resurrection power living in you, you too can dwell in the heights.

MALACHI

Yes, the King Is Coming!

When God's chosen people returned to Israel following their 70-year captivity in Babylon, they rebuilt the temple. They sought to obey Jehovah God and faithfully worshiped him. However, during the next one hundred years, they gradually became as evil as their ancestors. Apathy sucked their fervor of worshipping and obeying the Lord. Their economy was sick, their government corrupt and they were thumbing their noses at God. Israel was repeating the cycle of being faithful and then turning their backs on their covenant with God. His people turned from worshipping him to worshipping the gods of the nations around them.

This cycle is evident today as persecution of Christians increases. Cardinal Francis George has said, "I will die in bed, my successor will die in prison, his successor will die in the town square as a martyr and his successor will gather up the broken shards of civilization as has been the cycle of humanity since the beginning."

God's Love Is Present

God calls Malachi to awaken his relatives to open their eyes to their blind moral slide. Malachi begins by assuring them that God loves them. They asked cynically, "Really, how has God loved us?"

Malachi reminds them that God chose them. They were not destroyed like Jacob's twin brother, Esau, who came under God's wrath. (Mal. 1:2-3).

Israel's Priests Led Them Into Sin

The priests led the way to this moral slide. They showed contempt by offering God the castoffs from the flocks. "It is you, O priests, who show contempt for my name... You place defiled food (diseased food—blind and crippled and diseased animals) on my altar" (1:6-8). Their worship of God was a heartless, meaningless ritual, a burden rather than a joy. They were looking for a God of convenience. They wanted God's comfort and blessings without any accountability or commitment on their part.

God says, "If you do not listen, and if you do not set your heart to honor my name... I will send a curse upon you..." (2:1-2). "The lips of the priest ought to preserve knowledge, and from his mouth men seek instruction because he is the messenger of the Almighty. But you have turned from the way and by your teaching have caused many to stumble;..." say the Lord Almighty. (2:7-9). Ezra had the same problem: "The evil mindset spread to the leaders and priests and filtered down to the people - it kicked off an epidemic of evil, repeating the abomination of the pagans and polluting the Temple of God" (II Chron. 36:14 Msg.).

Many preachers are causing people to stumble as they present an unbalanced theology of grace and truth. Jesus' brother, James, writes, "Not many of you should presume to be teachers because you know that we who teach will be judged more strictly" (James 3:1). Today, pastors have lost the respect of the majority of the younger generation. Only one in three come to a pastor for guidance when they need help. More than half of American pastors admit to viewing porn at least monthly. Christianity Today reports that public trust in clergy has reached an all-time low. Americans put more trust in nurses, pharmacists, grade school teachers, medical doctors, military officers, and police officers than they put trust in the clergy.

More than half of today's pastors would change jobs if they could. Where is the burning passion, Jesus gave his disciples (Acts 4:20) or the passion of Paul who said, "I am compelled to preach? Woe to me if I do not preach the gospel" (I Cor. 9:16)? He preached with conviction. (I Thess. 1:5). Again, he says he is obligated to preach. (Ro. 1:14). Jeremiah says that God's word is like a fire shut up in his bones. He cannot keep it to himself. (Jer. 20:9). Paul admonishes us, "Never be lacking in zeal, but keep your spiritual fervor, serving the Lord" (Rom. 12:11). Have you lost your passion?

Violating God's Marriage Standards

The carnality of the priests led the people in their moral slide. "Judah has desecrated the sanctuary the Lord loves, by marrying the daughter of a foreign god. As for the man who does this, may the Lord cut him off from the tents of Jacob.... .2:11-12). Each of you men has been unfaithful to the wife you married when you were young. You promised that she would be your partner, but now you have broken that promise. Didn't God create you to become like one person with your wife? And why did he do this? It was so you would have children, and then lead them to become God's people. Don't ever be unfaithful to your wife. The Lord God All-powerful of Israel hates anyone who is cruel enough to divorce his wife. So, take care never to be unfaithful!" (Mal. 2:14-16 CEV).

The most prominent sin in the bible is sexual immorality, except for the sin of pride which is the root of all sin. It was only a few years before this that Ezra was beside himself when his people intermarried with the pagans around them. "The people of Israel... have not kept themselves separate from the neighboring peoples with their detestable practices, like those of the Canaanites.... They have taken some of their daughters as wives for themselves and their sons, and have mingled the holy race with the peoples around them. And the leaders and officials have led the way in this unfaithfulness. When Ezra heard this, he tore his tunic and cloak, pulled hair from his head and beard and sat down appalled" (Ezra 9:1-3).

Paul makes it clear that a follower of Jesus is not to marry a person who is an unbeliever. (I Cor. 7:39). But if you are a believer and you are married to someone who is an unbeliever you are to remain in the marriage if your partner is willing to live with you. (1 Cor. 7:12,13). If you are an unmarried Christian who is considering getting married to an unbeliever this is to be unequally yoked... What does a believer have in common with an unbeliever?" (2 Cor. 6:14). We see the pain of this unequal yoke in every church today. Spiritual unity between a believer and an unbeliever is lacking.

Before a young man proposes to his girlfriend, it is helpful to ask her parents if he can marry their daughter. If her parents are

Christian, they might answer, "Yes, if you promise you will love Jesus more than you love our daughter." (Matt. 6:33, 22:37-38). Divorce is all but eliminated when couples put God first. The same is true if you pray together - not just before meals but for your daily walk with God.

A Distorted View of God

The vast majority of Christians in America have an unbalanced view of God. God is love. His primary attribute is love. But God is also just, righteous and holy. David said, "You (God) hate all who do wrong" (Ps. 5:5). "Those who love violence he hates with a passion" (Ps. 11:5). "God's eyes are too pure to look on evil; he cannot tolerate wrong" (Habakkuk 1:13). God is a loving father, but he is also a just judge. Many Christians know John 3:16 where God loved us to the extent that he gave his only Son to save us from our sins. A few verses later, v. 36, we read: "whoever rejects the Son will not see life, for God's wrath remains on him." "The wrath of God is being revealed from heaven against all the godlessness and wickedness of people, who suppress the truth by their wickedness" (Ro. 1:18).

God's wrath and anger are mentioned nearly 500 times in the Scriptures, with 53 occurrences in the New Testament. Jesus rescues us from the coming wrath. (I Thess. 1:10). "Put to death... sexual immorality, impurity, lust, evil desires, and greed... because of these, the wrath of God is coming" (Colossians 3:5-6). The majority of Jesus' fifty-some parables refer to judgement. Many conclude with words such as, "they will be thrown into the fiery furnace where there will be weeping and gnashing of teeth, a phrase used by Matthew six times. Jesus says that if we bury our talents, we will be thrown into outer darkness. (Matt. 25:14:30).

America's god is a god of tolerance, so it is difficult to comprehend or believe in God as a just judge. (Rev. 19:2). God will judge his people with equity - with fairness, in righteousness. (Ps. 96:10, 13 and 97:2). God will not overlook sin unless it is under the blood of his dear Son Jesus. The vast majority of Christians in the United States cannot picture God meaning what he says when he speaks of justice and punishment.

Holiness vs. Justice/Truth

We forget that grace and truth are couplets which cannot be separated. "The Word (Jesus) became flesh and made his dwelling among us. We have seen his glory, the glory of the One and Only, who came from the Father, full of grace and truth" (John 1:14). Jesus came not only to demonstrate God's unlimited grace but also His absolute truth. "Grace and truth came through Jesus Christ" (John 1:17) God's Word is truth. (John 17:17). His truth will set you free. (John 8:36). If we reject God's truth, we suffer the consequences.

If we mention specific sins today, many Christians feel we are judgmental. "When you follow the desires of your sinful nature, the results are very clear: sexual immorality, impurity, lustful pleasures, idolatry, sorcery, hostility, quarreling, jealousy, outburst of anger, selfish ambition, dissension, division, envy, drunkenness, wild parties, and other sins like these. Let me tell you again, as I have before, that anyone living that sort of life will not inherit the Kingdom of God" (Gal. 5:19-21 NLT).

We act as if there are no essentials. We are afraid of words like diligence, effort, and obedience. We've downplayed verses that call us to work out our salvation with fear and trembling (Phil. 2:12) or verses that command us to cleanse ourselves from every defilement of body and spirit (2 Cor. 7:1) or warn against even a hint of immorality among the saints (Eph. 5:3).

Malachi Speaks to Robbing God

"Return to me, and I will return to you" 'says the Lord Almighty.'... "You have robbed me in tithes and offerings. You are under a curse... because you are robbing me. Bring the whole tithe... Test me...and see if I will not throw open the floodgates of heaven and pour out so much blessings that you will not have room enough for it" (Malachi 3:7-10).

An Abused Scripture

One of the most abused verses today is Luke 6:38: "Give, and it will be given to you. A good measure, pressed down, shaken together and running over, will be poured into your lap. For with the measure you use, it will be measured to you."

Taken in its context it is clear Jesus is not talking about giving money. He is talking about forgiving others. He says, "Don't judge... do not condemn... Forgive, and you will be forgiven" (v. 37). Jesus is instructing his followers to "give" forgiveness in the same amount we desire to be forgiven. We are to be as merciful as God is to us while judging, condemning and forgiving others in the same way we desire to be judged, condemned and forgiven by God.

New Testament Teaching on Giving

Paul instructs the Corinthians, "On the first day of every week, each one of you should set aside a sum of money in keeping with his income." (I Cor. 16:2). (1) We are to give individually. "Each one of you should set aside a sum of money in keeping with his income." (2) We need to give regularly, "On the first day of every week." (3) We give proportionately, "We give in keeping with our income." And (4) We give methodically, that is we have a plan we believe God desires for us to follow.

It's a joy to give. The important thing is that we see giving as a privilege and not a burden. It should not be out of a sense of duty, but rather out of love for the Lord and a desire to see His kingdom advanced. "It is more blessed to give to than receive" (Acts 20:35). Remember this: Whoever sows sparingly will also reap sparingly, and whoever sows generously will also reap generously. Each one should give what he has decided in his heart to give, not reluctantly or under compulsion, for God loves a cheerful giver" (II Cor. 9:6-7).

"God gives seed to farmers and provides everyone with food. He will increase what you have, so that you can give even more to those in need. You will be blessed in every way, and you will be able to keep on being generous. Then many people will thank God when we deliver your gift. What you are doing is much more than a service that supplies God's people with what they need. It is something that will make many others thank God. The way in which you have proved yourselves by this service will bring honor and praise to God. You believed the message about Christ, and you obeyed it by sharing generously with God's people and with everyone else. Now they are praying for you and want to see you because God used you to bless them so very much. Thank God for his gift that is too wonderful for words! (II Cor. 9:10-15 CEV).

Who has priority in your life, you or God? Is Christ really first—or do we put ourselves and our own desires first? Make sure Christ is first in your life. Ask God to guide you. "Whoever can be trusted with very little can also be trusted with much, and whoever is dishonest with very little will also be dishonest with much. So, if you have not been trustworthy in handing worldly wealth, who will trust you with true riches?... No servant can serve two masters. Either he will hate the one and love the other, or he will be devoted to the one and despise the other. You cannot serve both God and Money" (Luke 16:13).[29]

Faithfulness Is Rewarded

"Upon you who revere and worshipfully fear my name shall the Son of righteousness arise with healing in his wings... and you shall go forth like calves released from the stall and leap for joy. ... I will send you [John the Baptist in the spirit and power of] Elijah the prophet before the great and terrible day of the Lord comes. And he shall turn the hearts of the estranged fathers to the ungodly children, and the hearts of the rebellious children to their fathers lest I come and smite the land with a curse and a ban of utter destruction" (Mal. 3:16-4:6 AMP).

Malachi Anticipates God's Salvation

Malachi, as a final statement of judgment in the Old Testament, looks forward to God's saving work through the Messiah, Jesus Christ. The Israelites, descendants of Abraham, had the advantage of a rich history. Moses delivered them from slavery as God parted the Red Sea so they miraculously escaped from Pharaoh's army. Time and again he raised up judges, kings, and prophets to encourage and warn them to walk in God's will. Having all these advantages in their long history, the Israelites, seeing the rewards of

---

29 For additional information on "tithes" see the chapter on Abraham.

faithfulness and the punishments associated with judgment, still strayed from God's path.

This saga continues as 400 years later God sent the Messiah, his only Son Jesus, who was God in human form to show us how to live to please our Heavenly Father. It's through Jesus' sacrifice for our self-centered, stubborn nature that we are offered eternal salvation. It's through Jesus resurrection we conquer sin and death. When Jesus ascended to the Father, he did not leave us as orphans but sent his Holy Spirit to live in us enabling us to live holy lives as his ambassadors in this perverse world.

Will we ever learn? John answers that question as he describes the plagues of Revelations concluding with these words: "The rest of mankind that were not killed by these plagues still did not repent of the work of their hands; they did not stop worshiping demons, and idols of gold, silver, bronze, stone and wood—idols that cannot see or hear or walk. Nor did they repent of their murders, their magic arts, their sexual immorality or their thefts" (Rev. 9:20-21).

Nations come and go. Is there hope for the USA? God is not willing that anyone perish. (II Pet. 3:9). He calls you and me to be faithful in this wicked and perverse world. Jesus said there will be trouble as never before, "The heavenly bodies will be shaken. At that time, they will see the Son of Man coming in a cloud with power and great glory. When these things begin to take place, stand up and lift up your heads, because your redemption is drawing near." (Luke 21:28). "No eye has seen, no ear has heard, and no human mind has conceived, the things God has prepared for those who love him. (I Cor. 2:9).

Now glory be to God! By his mighty power at work within us, he is able to accomplish infinitely more than we would ever dare to ask or hope. May he be given glory in the church and in Christ Jesus forever and ever through endless ages. Amen" (Eph. 3:20-21 NLT).

Will you put your faith in Jesus and walk in obedience to his commands?

EPILOGUE

Hebrews 11 gives us a glimpse into the lives of men and women portrayed in "God's Hall of Faith." They were a small minority of faithful, no nonsense, followers of Jehovah God who were frequently misunderstood and persecuted. Their messages were recorded "to teach us, so that through endurance and the encouragement of the Scriptures we might have hope" (Romans 15:4).

The message of these men and women speak clearly to our current situation. Too often we set their message aside because we, like those they spoke to, don't want to hear of God's judgment. We want a "feel-good gospel" where sin is not taken seriously or completely overlooked.

Many of the popular preachers of America present a cheap grace—grace without repentance. God is not only a God of love and grace but also a God of righteousness, justice and truth. To present one without the other is an unbalanced gospel: a false gospel.

Hebrews 10:28-31, "If two or more witnesses accused someone of breaking the Law of Moses, that person could be put to death. But it is much worse to dishonor God's Son and to disgrace the blood of the promise that made us holy. And it is just as bad to insult the Holy Spirit, who shows us mercy. We know that God has said he will punish and take revenge. We also know that the Scriptures say the Lord will judge his people. It is a terrible thing to fall into the hands of a living God!" (CEV).

Thank God for his marvelous grace. We quote John 3:16-17, "For God so loved the world that he gave his only Son, that whoever believes in him shall not perish but have eternal life. For God did not send his Son into the world to condemn the world, but to save the world through him." But we must not stop there: "Whoever believes in him is not condemned but whoever does not believe stands condemned... Whoever believes in the Son has eternal life but whoever rejects the Son will not see life for God's wrath remains on him" (John 3:17 and 36).

The Church Has Lost Its Fire and Our Nation Has Lost Its Way

We are to walk in obedience to God and his Word. We are saved by faith - a faith that results in obedience. "Even the demons have faith, faith which is simply head knowledge without a heart change. (James 2:19). We are created by God for doing good works. (Eph. 2:8-10). "For as the human body apart from the spirit is lifeless, so faith apart from [its] works of obedience is also dead" (James 2:26 AMP). Jesus said, "Not everyone who says to me, 'Lord, Lord," will enter the kingdom of heaven, but only he who does the will of my Father in heaven" (Matt. 6:21). Unless we move from a "feel-good gospel" to the Gospel Jesus commissioned, i.e. making disciples, we will never hear Jesus' words, "Well done good and faithful servant" (Matt. 25:23).